"Charmingly uplifting, insightful an[...]
    John Gray, Ph.D., Author of "N[...]
    Women Are from Venus"

"A bold, witty and shamelessly fabulous must read for every single person on the planet!"
    Debbie Allen, Author of "Confessions of
    Shameless Dating"

"For the newly or about-to-be divorced, this book is an essential guide for dealing with the inherent unpleasantries with humor and insight. A great book for rising above the chaos."
    Diane DeLonzor, Author of "Never Be Late Again,
    7 Cures for the Punctually Challenged"

"This excellent book is long overdue. Anyone going through a divorce or continuing to make sense of the aftermath of a divorce will find this book highly empowering and enlightening. Tomi Tuel shows remarkable courage by sharing her valuable life lessons learned in the emotionally painful, chaotic trenches that all divorced individuals must struggle through. Every page delivers valuable and practical insights. Everyone dealing with divorce should have a copy of this book. Mental health professionals will do the right thing by recommending *101 Things I Learned After My Divorce* to any divorcing or divorced adults seeking to move on to better places."
    Jeffrey Bernstein, Ph.D., Author of
    "Why Can't You Read My Mind?"

"Tomi takes a positive, up beat and constructive approach to a subject that touches us all as we, our friends, our colleagues at work or our family members deal with the emotionally charged subject of divorce. Having been through a divorce personally, I was surprised to find myself laughing at old wounds that had never seemed all that funny before. This is a testament to the light yet deep approach taken in this highly useful book."

Stephen Lundin, Big Tuna Ph.D., Author of the four "FISH!" Books and Top Performer

"Tomi speaks from her heart allowing others to learn, forgive and move on. This book can help you heal and even love again…beginning with yourself."

Marcia Wieder – America's Dream Coach

"Inspiring and optimistic. This book is a breath of fresh air at a time when it is hard just to breathe. *101 Things I Learned After My Divorce* has the whole divorce recovery thing nailed. Clever, witty and full of real life vignettes is what makes this book a must have for anyone going through a divorce."

Roger Crawford, Author of the best seller "How High Can You Bounce?"

101 Things I Learned
<u>AFTER</u>
My Divorce

by Tomi Tuel

A STARJUNCTION BOOK

First Edition, March 2007

A *StarJunction Book*

This book's imprint is a registered trademark of StarJunction Books, a division of StarJunction International, Inc.

101 Things I Learned After My Divorce, by Tomi Tuel

Editor: Karen Conway

StarJunction Books trade paperback: ISBN 978-0-9790956-0-3
The Library of Congress has catalogued this edition as follows:
Tuel, Tomi, 101 Things I Learned After My Divorce
ISBN 978-0-9790956-0-3
1. Tuel, Tomi. 2. Self-help. 3. Divorce . 4. Happiness. 2007

PRINTED IN THE UNITED STATES OF AMERICA

5 4 3 2 1

To Jimmy and Erica,
bless your hearts.

I love you,
Mom

Contents

Foreword

THIS IS A TREASURE for anyone re-entering the world of dating – whether it is from divorce or any other relationship loss. I wish that I had this book years ago, as I would have recommended it to many patients in my practice: it is a humorous but direct accounting of the difficult situations and difficult feelings that are experienced when relationships dissolve.

As a psychologist in practice, I work with individuals every day who are experiencing relationship difficulties. Many don't recognize the difficulties in the relationship until it is over.

Tomi's book teaches us that relationship hindsights are less failures and more great opportunities to improve ourselves. Early in my career, a colleague of mine commented to me that each relationship is a "deeply held mirror". He was pointing out what Tomi is saying on each page: if you look carefully at your relationship, you will see where you can improve.

What is most valuable about this book is that it isn't just a guide on proper approaches to relationships – it is a very personal story that instructs. Because it is a personal accounting, we see ourselves in the vignettes, those things we wish we hadn't said or done. Unlike most of us, however,

Tomi admits them and instructs us from them. The added bonus is her humorous and amusing approach.

The only thing that you need to have in order to benefit from this book is relationship experience and an ability to enjoy. Tomi's description will make you laugh at the difficulties and nuttiness in all relationships, and she will show you how you can learn from them as well.

Daniel M. Rockers, Ph.D
Clinical Health Psychologist
Sacramento, California
May 2006

Acknowledgements

MY GRATEFUL ACKNOWLEDGEMENT GOES out to the following people:

My soul mate and husband, Todd Tuel, who gave me love and encouragement and brought excitement back into my life; who has endured paying for the mistakes of my ex with patience, love, and understanding; who fills my life with beauty, laughter, and romance; and who will be the one to love me as I grow old. I love you more than you will ever know.

My children, Jimmy and Erica, who without them I would not be complete; for their honesty and insightfulness; who have the ability to put things into perspective for me in a flash; whose tears and sadness through not understanding motivated me to tell my story; whom I have tried so hard to show that you can still be kind and work things out with an ex-spouse; who I hope will find their soul mates and have everlasting love in their own marriages someday; and who remind me of the innocence of childhood.

My sisters, Lorie, Suzanne, and Alene who have always been my biggest critics as well as my biggest supporters; for their interest in the book and their encouragement; for being my proofreaders and editors; for supporting me in the trenches of my divorce; and most of all, for knowing that I always had big sisters to stick up for me in times of trouble! I'd like to acknowledge them individually as follows: My oldest sister Lorie, for her wisdom and experience; for her ability to give it to me straight point of view; for her infectious laugh and humor; and for her true sense of understanding the pain of divorce. My sister Suzanne, the dentist, who always appreciates a full cookie jar; for her undying interest and collaboration in my project; for her business sense; for her generous parties; for all the laughter we shared over this project; and for being the first to say I will be on Oprah. My sister Alene, who lived 4 blocks from me and helped me on those nights I just needed a break; who always pulled through for me and delivered whatever the need, be it, her ability to recruit a van full of kids for a last minute birthday party, a drive to the store for medical supplies, or a moment's notice for company.

My parents, for giving me the constant security of family; for the role of what a mother and father should be; for their life long devotion to each other; for their ability to work together as parents to raise 4 teenage girls; for my parents' interpretation of what getting us to college really meant; for my mom's money management skills that got us there; for my dad's never ending patience to fix our cars so we literally could get there; for my privileged childhood full of fields to roam and polliwog ponds; for giving me a sense of being special; for their parental love; for making me proud of them and their special gifts; for the admiration, respect, and love bestowed on them from their life long friends; for instilling good health and nutrition in me at an early age; for setting standards and expectations that taught me discipline and perseverance; and for being the two people in my life I will feel I can never repay in so many ways, though I might try.

My cousin, Viki, who endured the heartache of divorce and was the first to embrace this book.

Mackie, our pound puppy who is a reminder that fate has a greater order for us all.

My ex-husband, Jim, who without the experience of divorce I never would have written about the subject. It forced me to look inward and grow. I'd like to thank him for our two children, who are beautiful in everyway; for going full-circle with me and my new husband; and for all the "I'm sorry's" that came later.

Diane Colson, my life long best friend whom I've known since Kindergarten; for never letting a day, or sometimes hour, go by without an email or phone call during my divorce; for never being too busy to offer an ear; for making growing up so much fun and humorous; for having a friend like you that I know so well, I can just look at you and laugh knowing something funny will come out.

Mike Dorsey, co-worker and life long friend who got me off my chair and taught me how to strut my stuff; for his humorous perspective and ability to make me find the humor in the raw stages of my divorce. Thanks for living the chump life together.

Jason Tomeda, co-worker who counseled me countless days. I am forever indebted.

Jim Pelley, childhood friend and lifelong, proclaimed adopted brother; who inspired this book and provided me humorous insight on so many issues. Because of your sharp wit and one-liners your presence always fills the room. Thank you so much for being my friend. I am so proud to know you.

Ronda Ellingsworth, respected lifelong friend and diehard running partner. A true femme who taught me everything I needed to know.

Lori Fox and Joe Lilley, for their encouragement and eagerness to help me in so many unexpected ways in my own self development.

Nicole Romeo, thank you for your enthusiastic nature and poetic gifts.

Laura Dupriest, respected friend who inspired me to write. Thank you for your encouragement and support.

Bill Marino, editor, mentor, book coach, and friend. Thank you for taking on this project. Your continued support and guidance, even in the rawest stages of this project, meant so much to me.

Jerry Mountjoy, managing editor by profession and respected literary mentor. Thank you for your professionalism and helping me to think outside of my trapezoid.

Karen Perrin, published freelance writer who read my work in its raw stages and still found it entertaining and insightful enough to read the entire book twice.

Ex-in-laws who were so supportive and didn't turn their backs; who still consider me family; and for being there when I needed you most.

Present in-laws who have welcomed me and my children into the family so genuinely, and who have always made my children and me feel special. I am so blessed to be a part of such a wonderful loving family.

Stories shared by all the survey participants. Without your stories I wouldn't have been able to drive the point home. Your stories made me realize just how common the pain of divorce is.

Computer Tech Tim Sutton, at the Computer Warehouse for saving my files I thought were lost forever.

Mike McMillin, owner of Laguna Preparers Service, you made the difficult legal process easy. Thank you for being patient and so matter of fact with me during a time when I couldn't decide if the hour was half past or half till.

Travis Wells, who gave me my first lesson in divorce recovery, which is consequently the introduction to this book.

Introduction

The Number One Thing I Learned After My Divorce

DIVORCE WILL BENCHMARK MANY of your life's future challenges. I now look at life this way: "Well hell, if I can get through a divorce, I can get through just about anything." It does that for you, but it also makes you realize – eventually – that there is always a brighter tomorrow, life does go on...and it really does only get better.

I didn't always feel this way. At first, I didn't think my life would ever be normal again. I didn't think I would ever feel joy when all I could feel was sorrow and sadness for myself and my two children. I was now on the dark side. I had somehow crossed over. My children were now *of* divorced parents. I no longer filed my tax return as "married filing joint." I had to get used to saying the "D" word.

In my early stages, admitting I was divorced bothered me. I would cringe at checking the "divorced" box on those marital status questions when filling out any kind of medical history at the doctor's office. It was like confiding that I was someone who didn't know how to work out relationship problems. I felt like that one word just said it all, "divorcee" (i.e. relationship loser). I could tell that even my widowed friends hated being confused for someone that was divorced. There seemed to be this unspoken stigma about being divorced even in this day and age.

Prior to my divorce I held a very narrow view of divorced people. When I was married I equated them to a different class, the "them's" and the "us's." I think a lot of married people who have never been divorced do subconsciously segregate people based on their relationship status. When I was married and everything was good, I didn't understand why people couldn't just work out their problems.

After I went through the initial detox phase of being separated, I did a great deal of self-reflecting on my failed marriage. It was then that I came to the conclusion that I didn't know it all. I was finding out that people who get divorced were no different from me. I later learned to embrace my new found marital status and changed my view of divorcees.

I found that there is an immediate bond shared by people who have been divorced. They are able to recognize what stage you are at in recovery quicker than others. They know your pain. People who have been through it (to hell and back) know that divorce is something you survive. They have an acute homing device that says, "Ah, there's one in trouble now." Suddenly the people who I thought needed to learn the most about relating were now my superhero mentors for survival.

I feel I have learned more of life's lessons than any university could ever teach me. Going through a divorce is a lot like enrolling in a crash course on emotional survival at the School of Hard Knocks. The difference is there is no grade at the end – it's a pass-fail course. And you don't have to pay tuition to attend. Don't get me wrong, you'll pay dearly for this education, but they don't call it tuition. The price of admission is a ticket for the emotional roller coaster — the ride of your life.

The School of Hard Knocks doesn't discriminate either. They will take anyone who applies. There is no instructor, no classroom, and no rules. There are definitely no rules. If you are confused and in need of help, you can explore your misunderstandings with a professional therapist. There are occasional tutors and other students in this lesson with which to share notes, but overall you are on your own for the comprehensive exam in life. It is a lesson learned alone.

1. Divorce opened my eyes spiritually, but the number one thing I learned after my divorce is that I have more to learn...

At the very beginning of my divorce, a good friend, who happened to be divorced himself, told me, "Everyone should experience a divorce once."

I looked at him baffled. "You're kidding, right?" I exclaimed. He insisted I hear him out. He told me, "You may think it's absurd now, but you will see what I mean." You will learn things about yourself and about others. You will learn how to appreciate the other person in your life more. You will relearn things you thought you already knew and your perspective will change."

I thought I knew it all. I didn't need to experience a divorce to learn to appreciate the other person in my life more. I already appreciated him. We didn't argue any more than other happily married couples we knew. We got along just fine – so I thought.

We all have a little bit of that seventeen year old kid still inside of us. At seventeen you aren't old enough to be an adult, but you sure think you know an awful lot. In fact, you even think you know more than most adults, especially your parents. Before my divorce I was kind of like that know-it-all seventeen year-old kid when it came to my marriage. Yogi Berra, the master at malapropism, said it best and his wisdom holds true for divorce: "It ain't over 'til, it's over"; "It's like déjà vu all over again"; and "You don't know what you don't know". Divorce was like that for me.

As the years passed, I remembered my friend's words. How true they rang! This is a book about what you will learn after experiencing a divorce. You will realize that divorce is about survival and when it is over you will be a different person. It will bring you deeper connections, with life and people that you never experienced before. You will journey to the ends of your comfort zone and realize that stretching your limits will be life altering.

You have been given a second chance, a do-over, a "Ctrl+Z" (undo). Most are unprepared for what lies ahead. After all, you didn't expect to wind up here – shattered dreams, disillusioned, overwhelmed, and alone. Although you can never be completely prepared for the future, I hope to provide you with insight as you re-enter single life.

This is a book about self-discovery, growth, and moving on after a divorce. The pages share my fears and foibles as well my rediscovery and renewal. My hope is you will find the calm in life that comes after obtaining inner-peace with your new circumstance. I hope to get you closer to that point through the laughter and tears this book may invoke.

So much is written about recovering from loss, but little about the very real experiences during the process of divorce. I want to change that with this book. I hope that you will see reflections of your own experiences in these pages and find my words both helpful and comforting in getting you through the next stages of your life. It is also my hope that through humor you will be transformed as I was and gain a sense of serenity and renewed wholeness that allows you to embrace your new life as it begins to unfold. I wish you the best in your journey through life after divorce!

Now that you have applied to the University of Hard Knocks let's get started on your degree. Join me for the lesson of your life. The School of Hard Knocks is in session and class is about to begin…

1

The Definition of Divorce

I RECENTLY READ THAT ONLY two percent of American adults have parents that are still alive and married to each another. I'm one of the fortunate two percent, but my children are not. Divorce has had an impact, in some way or another, on most of our lives, but what does it really mean? The American Heritage dictionary defines the noun divorce as:

1.The legal dissolution of a marriage. 2. A complete or **radical separation** of things closely connected, from the verb "vorced."

Yeah, it's a radical separation alright. Separation from your pension, your house, your family, your dreams, just about everything and everyone you love. Yes, divorce is a radical separation of things closely connected. Our lives become intertwined through marriage. We take our vows, "Till death do us part" and it is only natural to assume our marriage will last forever. And when it doesn't, separation from even the smallest things seems radical. The dictionary goes on to define the verb "divorce" as:

1. To dissolve the marriage bond between. 2. To shed (one's spouse by legal divorce). 3. To separate or remove, disunite.

Is anyone else thinking what I'm thinking? What the heck does it mean *"to shed one's spouse"*? I always thought of shedding as something my dog does. "To shed (one's spouse…)" Definitions like that make marriage and people seem so disposable. Like a Dixie cup. "Okay, I'm done with you, so ta-ta. I'm shedding you now. Bye-bye, in the trash you go." This defining verb, "to shed," equates divorce to snake-like behavior, but as unscrupulous as it may sound, this definition is fitting in some cases. Take the infamous Henry the VIII, who, after tiring of a wife, would "shed" her. Only he didn't divorce his wives; he had them beheaded.

I think if I had to define "divorce" in my own words, it would be more like this: 1. a pain in the ass, in the heart, and in the wallet. 2. From the adjective "sucky." There's not a whole lot more to say about divorce than that.

Statistically, divorce will drop your wealth an average of 77%. As a divorced person, you lose economies of scale with living expenses and investments. What were once shared expenses, between presumably two incomes, are now essentially double.

It's definitely not a pleasant part of any relationship or life. But, like a lot of things, divorce has to be experienced to be fully appreciated. After you've gone through one, unless you're a complete dummy, you will come away with a better understanding of life, and the big picture.

My all-time favorite divorce-related word is "estranged." It's from the Latin word extraneare, which conveniently is also embedded in the word "extraneous." Estranged? What a wacky word. It's usually used during the separation phase of a divorce to describe someone's husband or wife. *Strange*, hum. A more fitting word to describe spousal behavior during this time, don't you think? So why don't people just say what they really mean. "It's not someone's 'estranged' husband (or wife); it's his or her 'strange' husband (or wife)." That would make more sense to everyone and provide a partial excuse for why someone going through a divorce is acting so peculiar.

FROM THE TUELBOX

Take note. Divorce is a radical separation. If you are contemplating divorce or just want to quantify the experience, however difficult or "sucky" you *think* divorce will be, take that number and multiply it by the rotation of the earth, then hang on!

2

Trying to Move Rainbows (My Story)

RAINBOWS ARE BEAUTIFUL. THEY have a sense of glory and provide hope for a brighter tomorrow. Rainbows can be seen for miles around, but no matter how hard you try, you will never find their beginnings or ends. When you are in the middle of one with your eyes wide open, you don't even know it's there. Rainbows are weightless, but they cannot be lifted, pushed, or inverted.

Relationships are a lot like rainbows. For many of us, it's hard to remember exactly when our relationships began and when they ended. Sometimes, we don't even realize we are in the middle of something glorious until it is too late. Our eyes may be wide open, but our minds are closed to the beauty in our partners. Often times in my own life, I felt I was trying to move rainbows alone. I didn't understand why it didn't work; I just knew I wasn't getting anywhere.

We all have a story to tell. This is mine. I met my ex-husband, Jim, at junior college. I was just 23 and had already earned a four-year degree in Business. We met in an accounting class that I was taking as a refresher for my Master's degree. Gifted with numbers, Jim was quite the center of attraction for a few girls in the class, including me. He was young, a beach blonde, and very tan from working that summer for his father's concrete company. On top of that, he was pulling straight As in a class that I was repeating. When he wound up sitting next to me in class, I got the chance to get to know him, and nine months later we were engaged.

Our engagement would last another nine months, then after knowing each other barely a year-and-a-half, we were married. I was 24, he was 29. I continued to pursue my master's degree, while he eventually lost interest and quit attending college altogether.

2. Bait and Switch - Changing the educational game plan midstream is a bunch of crap.

I remember feeling a little slighted when Jim announced that he didn't want to go back to school. I didn't understand. School was so easy for him, and I knew how hard I had worked for my degree. To see someone with that much potential just quit was upsetting on many levels. The gap between us professionally began to widen. He was content to be a physical laborer, while I saw him as a numbers guy in the corporate world.

He continued in construction while I pursued a career, but his desire to start a family right away became the first challenge to our marriage (and there were many). I was hell bent on getting my degree, but I compromised, thinking I could do both. After all, getting a master's would only take two years. It would be a cinch – so I thought!

The first three years of our marriage, we lived in a log cabin in a small town called Sutter Creek in the California foothills. We were on a mountain, 12 miles from town, in a 600-square foot log cabin that was so old, the chinking in the logs and around the windows was starting to crumble. On a windy day, the curtains inside the house would blow, even when the windows were shut. The cabin was actually a historic home and it belonged to his parents. It had been built before the turn of the century and was constructed from the trees on the land. It sat in a peaceful meadow on eight acres. Down from the house was a pond and every spring the turtles came to sun themselves. Autumns were pretty. The many oaks on the property would undress themselves of their golden-red leaves, completely changing the scenery. Winters were cold and our only source of heat was a wood burning stove.

We had no garbage service out where we were. Every couple of months or so we hauled our horse trailer, what we used for our dumpster, off to the local dump. In the summer months, the smell of the horse trailer could get pungent. In the fall, leaf burning was an acceptable practice and was necessary for fire safety. The smell would give me a headache. Stacking firewood was one of my summertime jobs. I didn't mind it, until one day after stacking wood I found a tick buried in my back.

Because we were so far from town, I used to do my marketing only twice a month. I remember one time my niece and nephew came to visit us one summer. Like kids do, they made themselves some snacks one afternoon. Instead of making themselves sandwiches, they ate just the lunch meat without any bread. I remember how I jumped on them. I told them, "We make meals around here because it is twelve miles to the nearest store." My nephew made the revelation, "That's 24 miles round trip!"

Our pipes were full of rust and the house was unlevel, but for a pair of newlyweds this was an adventure – at least for me it was. For Jim, it had been the house he was raised in. It was here he spent his formative years and it was here he wanted to die. He was used to this lifestyle. I grew up on three acres with all the barnyard animals you could imagine. I was not unfamiliar with chores, but I wasn't accustomed to roughing it and being isolated.

I had no friends or family nearby, every phone call I made incurred long distance charges, and the closest mall was over an hour away. These were important to me at twenty-four. My idea of living in the country was being 50 yards away from the city limit.

Because we had so much land, it became the family dumping ground. After awhile I got used to the gutted out greyhound bus, the dismantled trucks and the empty trailers that became landmarks for the occasional visitor. At that time in Sutter Creek, I felt like a city girl living like a hillbilly.

Our first born came after two years of marriage. I was twenty-six. We had a boy and amazingly he was born on Jim's thirty-first birthday. But, as much as I loved staying home with my new baby, I was career-oriented and felt time was getting away from me. I knew the statistics: the longer you are out of school, the harder it is to go back. I was afraid if I waited too long, I would never get my master's degree.

When I was five-and-a-half months pregnant I lost my job as a graphic illustrator, shortly after that my application to the university's graduate program was rejected, and for the first time in my life I had no direction. I relied on my husband to support me. Jim didn't mind, but it went against my upbringing. I didn't like being financially dependent.

If school taught me anything, it was that red tape is made to be cut and "no" was never the final answer. I persisted in getting into the university. After letters and the approval of the academic advisory committee, I was admitted, conditionally. I could not be on academic probation more than three times. That meant I could not drop my GPA below a B average. I was finally able to start the Master's program when my son was three months old.

After all my pleading to be accepted to the university, I was placed on academic probation twice within the first three semesters (one more time and I would have been disqualified for good). I completely withdrew one semester due to illness and to avoid the possibility of facing my third and final probation notice. My immune system was low due to stress and I seemed to catch every strain of flu my son was exposed to in daycare.

As a young couple with a small child trying to get ahead in life, we were like two ships passing in the night. Jim would get home at 3 p.m., after making the hour-long commute from work in Sacramento, and I would turn around and make that same trip back to make my 5 p.m. class at the University. Our day started and 4 a.m., mine to study and Jim's to get ready for work, it made for a long day.

With every semester came a new scheduling challenge. Sometimes I wouldn't be so lucky and the 5 pm class wouldn't be available, or I might have to attend classes five days a week, instead of two or three – it would just depend. During the fall months, I had to be mindful of the tulle fog on the one lane highway at night and would try to schedule my classes early.

3. Ultimatums are the control freak's way of reaching a compromise.

It was during this time I convinced Jim (or rather insisted) that we move from the foothills to Sacramento. It only made sense to me to move closer to Sacramento to simplify our lives. I wanted to be closer to school and for Jim to be able to spend more time with our son. This request nearly caused us to divorce. You would have thought I had asked him to give up his right testicle. He didn't want to move to the city, but he eventually succumbed. In retrospect, this was the beginning of the end.

Most bad relationships seem to have one resounding issue that comes up whenever there is an argument. Ours was the new house. I loved it; he hated it. To me, it was ideal: close to his work and my school, in a great school district, and just a few blocks from my sister. Best of all we were five minutes from the mall!

After being isolated on a mountaintop for three years, it was a welcome change for this city girl. But Jim felt he had been forced to move, and he wanted to be back on the mountain in the little log cabin. I felt strongly about buying a house. To me, there was a certain order in life: school, marriage, house, and then baby. Only, in our case the baby came before the house. If I had only known then what I know now, I might not have given him the ultimatum to move. I would have been more relaxed, but it was a crazy time.

Because we bought a house, I had to get a job. I eventually landed two part-time jobs and, at one point, was also serving an unpaid internship. I was always stressed because for part of this time our family had no medical benefits. Finally after a year of temp jobs, I got hired as an analyst for the state when I was twenty-eight and began my career.

It was the early 1990s and his parent's concrete business had just succumbed to the slump that hit the California real estate market. Jim felt obligated to help his parents out of their financial situation, but starting a new concrete business required a large outflow of cash which we didn't have. By the time he was through incurring debt you could have played a hand of poker with all our credit cards. Jim was running his own concrete business, but he was struggling to make it work. To his credit he stuck it out, but we were buried up to our eyeballs. I pleaded with him many times to cut his losses and close the business, but that didn't happen until things were much worse for us financially.

I could not see how to help Jim with his business. If I quit my state job, we would lose all of our medical benefits, and Jim simply didn't make enough to pay the way for both of us, let alone cover the costs of a medical plan. After awhile he stopped taking a paycheck just so he could pay his employees. I needed to stay focused on completing my degree and keeping my job. The hardest part was, we had been okay financially before he started his own business. Before the concrete business, I was making enough money that he could have just worked part-time and finished the degree he started when I met him. That was what *I* wanted for him; I didn't want him to struggle, but it wasn't what *he* wanted.

I had a college deadline to meet. Most people don't know this, but after seven years, graduate classes in the California State University System expire *(per CA Regulations code section 40510)*. If you have not completed your degree within that timeframe, your classes begin to disappear from your transcript, one by one, as if you never took them. It's like the movie *Back to the Future*, when one by one Michael J. Fox's family members disappear from the photograph. The seven-year rule is only an issue when life intervenes. Most people who don't quit or drop out can complete a degree in that amount of time. When I first heard about the seven-year rule, I remember thinking, that would never happen to me; you'd have to be some kind of bozo to be around that long!

Along the way, we became resentful of each other. Go figure. I wanted to simplify our lives while accomplishing my academic goals, but Jim didn't see any benefit in it for him. In fact, he often told me how spoiled I was because I was doing what I wanted to do. Somehow he thought I was having fun, running at full speed to get everything done by the deadline. Meanwhile, I thought he was putting up obstacles for me.

Fast forward five-and-a-half years. It was a tough road, but I finally finished the course work for my master's program. However, I was not as excited as I thought I would be. I finished a week earlier than everyone else because I was expecting my second child any day. Relieved was probably a better way to describe my emotions at that time. Still working for the state, I had great leave benefits and a great retirement, but Jim's concrete business was plummeting. He took a second job just to make ends meet.

Out to here and burnt out on school, I still had a thesis to write, but that would wait. I would fit that in somewhere between attending an audit academy for my state job with the tax agency, studying for the CPA exam, and taking care of a newborn. After another grueling year, my thesis was approved and finalized. I was now 32. What I thought would take me two years took nearly seven. Life intervened, and I was that bozo!

Now, like most recent college graduates, I had to learn how to relax. For years it was go, go, go; even when I had a break, I was studying for a test. Now I was finally able to sit and watch a television show from start to end, or read a book for pleasure, if I wanted. But I didn't do any of those things. Instead, I continued full-steam ahead, studying for the CPA exam. Not being able to fully relax, I drove Jim nuts, and I knew it. He must have thought I would be this way forever.

I took the CPA exam and didn't pass. My mother told me to take some time off to just be a mom. Woo-hoo! I had the parental okay to stop. I could finally take a guilt-free break from the school crazies. I was just beginning to wind down from everything, when the next wave of my life hit.

During the time when Jim took on the second job, he never slept more than two hours at a time. This went on for nearly a year. I worried about his health. The effects of sleep depravation can be fatal, and he didn't look good. He didn't need to work so much, and I pleaded with him to cut back, but it fell on deaf ears. I began to feel like he preferred working to being home.

In the midst of all the working, studying and child-rearing, there was nothing to keep our marriage strong. Our sex life was non-existent. When we did have time for each other he was too tired. He preferred staying home to going out.

Then, something happened that made me think things were going to get better. Jim closed the concrete business, and after much convincing, came to work with me for the state. Life would be great. We would have the same holiday schedule, money would be steady, he could quit his part-time job, and our lives would be easier – even normal. The best part, at least for me, was we were working for the same agency and in the same building. I thought I would get to spend more time with him, but that's when he met her.

Jim was the quiet type around the ladies. It was part of his charm, I suppose. An aggressive woman could make child's play of Jim. He went from working in a male-dominant profession to a female-rich environment. It had to have been sensory overload for him. He was climbing the ladder quickly and became a trainer – the center of attention among the ladies. Jim ate it up.

One woman in particular over-stepped her boundaries. Her name was LaRonda. She was eight years his senior, tall, thin, and with long blonde hair. At 44, her looks were defused by her lack of happiness. A struggling single mother, left to care for her two children on her own (children who were now in their late teens), she lived in a small apartment and worked the night shift with Jim.

Although Jim and I worked in the same building, we seldom saw each other because I worked during the day. At the end of my work day, he would meet me in the parking lot with the kids in the car. He would jump out and go to work, and I would get in the car and take the kids home. He would drive my car home after work. It seemed to be working. We were saving on daycare expenses, and soon he'd be able to quit his midnight to 4 a.m. job for the newspaper.

4. If the only time you have to work on your relationship is at work, then you better be married to your job; otherwise, forget about it.

After his first month working for the state, I asked him when he planned to quit his other job. We didn't need the money anymore. I was shocked when he told me he wanted to keep that job. I didn't understand it, at least not at first. Years later, a friend put it this way, Jim was never at home, he was always working and the only time he had for a relationship was while he was at work.

I began to get suspicious when I never saw any paychecks from the newspaper job. I became doubly suspicious when one day I got to the mail first. There was a bank statement for an account in his name that I had not seen before. I asked him about it later. With his back to me, he said, "Oh, I told you I was going to open an account." Now, that might have worked if the subject were stopping after work for a beer or inviting the neighbors over for football, but the flippin' subject was a checking account! Back the truck up! That's something I would remember. I protested, "You never told me anything about opening a checking account without my name on it. What's going on?" He played it cool but was emphatic he had told me. I temporarily dropped the issue.

Questions flooded my mind. Was he even working a second job? I had no proof; I never saw a single paycheck since he supposedly started the job four months before. I had relinquished the household budget to him long ago. It was too hard for me to keep track of his ATM transactions, so I threw up my hands and let him handle it. It was one less thing for me to worry about while I was in school.

He began acting strange and distant. Sometimes, when the kids were at daycare, I would visit him at work, but he seemed angry that I was there. I didn't understand it. I didn't know she was watching. On weekends, he would leave for hours, telling me he was with an old high school buddy. I knew he only kept in touch with one friend from high school, and this was not him. After nine years together (seven-and-a-half years of marriage), you know each other's friends.

Once when I came home from work he was on the phone with someone, but he hung up immediately, saying that he would call them back later and acting as if he needed to talk to me. But he said nothing. He just hung up and went back to what he was doing. Odd, I thought.

After two months of feeling like I was nothing more than an irritation, I told him to leave and go find himself. During the two weeks he was gone, I found out about the other woman from a co-worker. Two months later, I filed for divorce. Another six months (California's compulsory cooling-off period) and our divorce was final. Three weeks later, Jim and LaRonda were married. Six months after that they were divorced, but they would remain together for the next five and a half years; and eventually, they both left the department where I was working.

5. When you let your ex back into your life before you have dealt with the issues, you will split up a second time and relive your divorce all over again. It is hard on you, but harder on your children.

Jim and I tried to reunite during their separation, it didn't last a week. I opened my heart up to him because he said he was truly sorry. By all appearances he was. Kleenex tissue was not enough. The tears he cried required a dishtowel. However, by the third day he switched gears. He couldn't leave her and ended up going back. That was it for me. I couldn't put the kids or myself through something like that ever again. For the duration of their relationship (5 ½ years on and off), Jim's life with her was a living hell, until they finally split for good.

Our divorce was pretty standard. We fit the classic text-book statistics. Most men divorce at age 36 and remarry within one year. Most women; however, take five years to remarry. Most couples get back together at least one time for a final try before ending the relationship for good. I remember reading this statistic at the very beginning of my divorce and was astonished how I could, with certainty, predict our fate. He confessed to me once that he didn't know how to be alone, but he couldn't decide between me and his new girlfriend. The irony is that, in the end, he had neither of us in his life and he was alone.

Our divorce was relatively simple. I used a paralegal to file; he used an attorney, but for the most part, he gave me what I asked for, probably out of guilt. For that, I thanked him. We didn't have a huge estate nor a drawn-out divorce fought by attorneys. It was quick and simple, but I still felt a hundred years older when it was over.

I floundered for the next two years, trying to pick up the pieces of my life and become indifferent towards Jim. It took five years to go full circle and reach a point where we could be friendly toward each other with no animosity.

Today, we have the ideal divorce – from time to time. We are involved in each other's daily lives, because of the kids. We share everything about them. It's not about anything else anymore. Jim now has someone new in his life, and I embrace her.

I met my current husband, Todd, after I had closure with Jim, but long before I felt indifferent. Todd was my "Someday Man"—the one all my friends said would come along, someday. He was my "knight in shining armor," and he helped rejuvenate my soul. We met two years after Jim left and married five years after my divorce was final. We

currently live just ten minutes from Jim's house. Because
Todd is very secure in our marriage, he understands my relationship with Jim as the father of my children. Todd and Jim
get along, and I couldn't ask for a better spouse. I'm the
happiest I have ever been and consider myself one of the
lucky ones because I had it to do over again and found my
soul mate in the process.

FROM THE TUELBOX

I think we all go down the same road in life at various
stages of our marriages. For some, it's a lazy path; for other's,
it's a frickin' superhighway. In the beginning of a marriage
we all start down that path of 110% commitment. Then, just
when you think the relationship is on cruise control and
you're searching for a rainbow, the one riding shotgun calls
out, "Go left!" The relationship heads south, and depending
on the speed at which you are traveling, you may arrive in
Divorceville sooner than you expect.

But, for those of you directionally challenged, just
remember: you didn't get here alone – perhaps you had
someone riding shotgun that couldn't read the marriage
compass!

3

The Hardest Part
About Getting Divorced

HOW MANY TIMES HAVE you been mad at your spouse and secretly wondered what it would be like to be single again? Most of us have toyed with the idea at one time or another. I suspect most people who are reading this book took action on those thoughts. It happens like this: you are still there physically, but you have checked out mentally. Perhaps the thought crossed your mind after putting all the dishes away, only to find the kitchen a mess just an hour later, or searching for something you need, like a pair of scissors, and finding them broken or dirty and not in their proper place.

We all experience these little nuisances at one time or another. It's normal to wonder what it would be like to always find things where you left them, and in the condition you left them. But these are little things, and most of us would never seriously think of leaving our spouses over them.

Sometimes these thoughts can be fleeting. In a flash, you may recount the blessings of your marriage and can be humbled by an act of kindness, like when you are presented with a vase full of fresh-cut flowers. Only then, do you realize how lucky you are to have someone who, in their excitement to please you, flung open the cupboards, cut the flowers with your favorite scissors, and didn't put these things away.

Your frustrations melt away and you are humbled by their act of kindness. It's these acts of kindness that are key; simple gestures that bring us toward one another and back to the relationship.

HOW DOES A MARRIAGE BREAK DOWN?

What happens first? Do we lose the ability to counter the little frustrations with loving thoughts, or do the loving acts toward one another cease? No one really knows. It can happen gradually and sneak up on a marriage. Marriage is as much mental as it is physical. When we focus on the love and not the little nuisances, we continue to promote loving acts. Instead of getting mad about things not being tidy, we need to remind ourselves how lucky we are to have someone special in our lives.

But let's not kid ourselves; there isn't always a good reason for the annoying things. When no good reason for the inconsiderateness can be found, then you have two choices to make. You can continue to be peeved and keep it bottled up inside, or you can let it out creatively. If you are always getting ticked off at your partner, it takes work and imagination to change your way of thinking. You have to be creative and find the humor in the process.

For example, my current husband is a daredevil. It never fails that he will put himself at risk of injury whenever we go on vacation. I know this about him, so whenever we go somewhere, I make sure to bring some Vicodin from his last maneuver, just in case. We have, what seems like, a revolving prescription for anti-inflamatories and painkillers. I never tell him I have it, until he's done something stupid. Then suddenly I'm his hero. We affectionately refer to the money used to cover the expenses from his little mishaps as the "Dumbass Fund."

On our last vacation, we went to the Hawaiian island of Maui. We took the winding, coastal road to Hana, a tropical paradise featuring some of the most beautiful sights I have ever seen. Along the way, we passed tropical rainforests and many waterfalls. At one stop Todd decided to jump off a four-story tall waterfall. I wasn't amused. Help was a long way away. When he hit the water, the impact broke his tailbone. He started to bruise immediately and gingerly made his way back to the car. By the end of our vacation, the bruise was the size of a baseball above his butt crack. Now every time he tells the story, I laugh and say, "The bruise wasn't really from the jump; it was from my foot after he did it!"

When we lose the ability to counter our frustrations with loving thoughts, or fail to find the humor in situations, we develop a negative vision. If left unchecked that negativity can destroy a relationship and result in a divorce. Replace those goggles that have blinded you with your polarized shades, my friend. Search for the beauty in your differences. When the loving thoughts and acts of kindness have ended and your answer is divorce, then listen up. You've got more to learn about coping, and divorce is the sink-or-swim method by which you will learn.

6. You can get through anything if you can eventually find the humor in it.

Let's face it. Things aren't always funny when you are going through a divorce, but it is your job to eventually find the humor in some of it. One of my sisters would tell me to visualize the one who hurt me being in some kind of naked predicament. If a guy dumped me, she would say, "Picture him naked and then use your imagination." It's kind of immature, but it helps when you add something like "behind bars." to the end of your visualization. You can have fun with this. You can have several different taglines. Some of my favorites are: "on a crowded street," "in front of a cop," "during a fire drill", "running out of gas", "on Mt. Everest without a jacket." You get the picture.

So let's just say your spouse comes to you on that fateful day and tells you, "Dear, I just don't love you any more." This is not funny to you, yet. It's still too raw, but after a few months pass and the shock has had time to set in, you may find yourself laughing about it. In fact, you may try to role play and re-enact the scene. And after a few shots of Tequila it will be hilarious!

7. Stay close to friends sharing similar experiences in their life…you will find humor in each other's circumstances.

Sometimes the best way to find the humor in your situation is with friends going through similar situations. It's the old adage: misery loves company. Friends who shared similar experiences with me during this time brought me comfort. If anyone could relate, they could. We would make each other laugh at the rawness of our wounds. It was healing, to say the least.

Sometimes your problems pale in comparison to theirs and in a shallow way, it will lift your spirits. You share a bond. It's called the bond between two chumps. Not only do you feel like chumps, but you are living the chump life. Friends like this instantly know when something has happened. Sometimes all you have to do is give them "the look," while shaking your head, and they know your pain.

Being able to laugh at your ex helps when you give them a nickname. Chump friends are very clever at this game. One of my chump friends loved to use Disney characters as nicknames. Two of my favorites were Tweedle Dee and Tweedle Dumb. Whenever Jim and LaRonda did something that I disagreed with, my chimp friend would say: "That's just Tweedle Dee and Tweedle Dumb for you." Then we would in unison say, "Doh, Doh, Doh!" – and it would make me laugh.

Endorphins generated through laughter have amazing healing power. Laughter is key! Let me show you what I mean. According to Prevention Magazine, a new study conducted by the University of Maryland Medical Center showed that laughter can lead to a healthier heart by improving blood flow. Other medical journals purport that when we laugh we:

- Alleviate depression;
- Lower our blood pressure;
- Promote relaxation;
- Reduce stress;
- Increase the oxygen level in our blood, giving us more energy;
- Increase the endorphin activity in our body resulting in a sense of well being;
- Are able to keep things in perspective
- Banish boredom;
- Are more socially attractive – people enjoy being with those who laugh easily and often; and
- Immeasurably increase our enjoyment of life.

Having a support group of friends is the best heart medicine I know. One day I had coffee with a few of my divorced friends. We all compared notes on how we each had dealt with fits of anger during our divorces. One person shared his solution to punching holes in the wall. Instead of throwing punches he threw rolled up socks. The visual alone of this 6'3" ex-linebacker throwing socks was a sight to behold. This triggered my other friend to admit she pitched her cell phone over a bridge when her ex was hounding her. My other friend convinced he was above the conversation, offered no antidote. So we roused him until he finally admitted he had a weenie roast with all their old love letters. He chimed in, "And you want to know something? They were the best wieners I ever had."

THE NO FAULT DIVORCE

I have always thought it amazing that both parties in a divorce usually feel they have been wronged – no matter who left whom. Like many injustices we experience, we want the world to know it wasn't our fault. Unfortunately, there is no way to place legal blame in California and many other states. I remember how mad I was when I started filling out the paperwork to file for divorce. I kept looking for the box that said "Cheater" or "Adulterer," but the only choices were "Irreconcilable Differences" or "Annulment." I wanted to blame him, and there were no categories for that. I felt gypped.

At least in car accidents you have the choice of no-fault or you can cast 100 percent of the blame on the poor fool that rear-ended you. Not so in divorce, even though I sure felt like I had been rear-ended. It's a little ironic. A total stranger can rear-end you by accident, and you can sue him for damages. Depending on the circumstances you can put him in the poor house, take his license away, and ruin his driving record if he is found at fault. But your own spouse can ruin you financially, devastate you emotionally, and turn your world upside down, and you can't even legally have the satisfaction of blaming him for causing you so much pain and anguish. You don't get to legally say it was *his fault* or *her fault*. Instead you have to check the box that says "Irreconcilable Differences" (code words for: *OUR FAULT*)! I hated this description because it made me feel like I was somehow responsible for the divorce, when he was the one who left. I was mad about that at first; Why should I be blamed for something I didn't do? I hadn't learned yet how I had contributed to the divorce.

In the end, you find out it doesn't help to try to blame the other party. You both suffer financially, emotionally, and in many other ways no matter who or what caused the divorce. What is needed is no-fault divorce insurance: something to protect you against the ensuing damages. But I'm here to tell you, you are your own best insurance plan.

HOW WE CONTRIBUTE TO
THE RELATIONSHIP'S END

We generally have a keen sense of what ended the marriage, but do we really give much thought to how we contributed to the relationship's end?

8. One of the hardest things about getting divorced is accepting your part in it.

We are always quick to blame the other person and focus our attention on what *they* did wrong. But that doesn't really matter anymore. *They* are gone. What matters most is figuring out what your role was in the marriage's failure. In very subtle ways, we have defining contributions to its end. And we can miss it entirely if we're not paying attention.

As I mentioned in chapter 2, I was very driven to get a master's degree. I look back on how I could have changed things and where I went wrong in my marriage. Perhaps I married Jim too soon. In my mind, I was not supposed to get married until after I finished my four year degree. Though it was never spoken, my parents expected that. Once married, I was off the 'mom and dad payroll' and had to support myself. A master's degree was not expected of me and so I somehow felt I had achieved the parental approval and could approach the higher education on my terms. That's why I felt it was time to get married.

Jim and I only knew each other a year and a half before we were wed. At 24 I barely knew who I was. I didn't know if I was particularly creative or intellectual. I had few opinions about things and had no interest in current events. I thought because Jim was 5 years older than me he would have a direction soon. I expected a lot of him because I expected a lot from myself. The opposite was true of Jim. He didn't expect anything from me, perhaps because he wanted a simple life. We both had 20/20 eyesight, but we didn't share the same vision.

Had I known better who I was, I would have had a better idea of who I was suppose to marry. I think Jim always felt the pressure of my expectations and got tired of trying to meet them. But my expectations were not out of line. I expected to live somewhere close to a town, with decent plumbing, and dependable electricity. I expected him to have a 9 to 5 job and a retirement plan. If something major broke I expected to have the money available to fix it. I took an oath for better or for worse, and was fully committed to the struggle. I figured eventually we would achieve these ideals.

One of the hardest things about getting divorced is the growing pains you go through figuring all this out and seeing how you helped cause your own divorce. This is also the lesson that takes the longest to learn. You never fully understand it until you are in another long-term, loving relationship, and someone new points out your relationship flaws. Only then do you have a clue, but it still comes in phases and takes time.

9. There is a difference between communicating and grunting.

Even if you know your relationship is headed south, the $60 million question is: how do you get a non-communicator to tell you what's wrong? You've got nothing to work with if all you get from them is, "I'm not happy," and they can't tell you why, a tangible why. They might as well be grunting at you.

As much as we would like to, we can't torture them to spill it. Tying your spouse to a chair in a smoke-filled room under a spotlight, while you stand holding a baton is not an option. You cannot force someone to talk. Some people are not self-reflective and live simply in the moment. They know they are unhappy, but they can't tell you why. But without any information, you cannot change any of your ways or see how you are contributing to the problem. When this happens and your spouse is unwilling to seek counseling, there is little you can do. You cannot be blamed for that.

10. One of the hardest things to come to terms with is admitting to yourself that everyone else was right about the two of you not being right for each other.

Some people are just not meant to be together. In my early twenties, I barely had an opinion about anything. As a result, I was attracted by looks and brawn. So it was not surprising that as I grew older and began developing my own interests, I realized I had very little in common with my husband. It is hard to admit to yourself that you were wrong about the person you married or that you married for the wrong reasons. Worse yet, perhaps you weren't as ready for marriage as you thought you were.

GETTING TO KNOW THE LEGAL PROCESS

11. The hardest part about getting divorced wasn't the paperwork.

That was actually the easiest part. Deciding to get divorced was much harder. I vacillated back and forth. I was so indecisive during that time. Fortunately, I had a wonderful paralegal to help me through it.

12. Get someone with patience and a take-charge attitude to handle your divorce.

One day I would want the divorce; the next day I wouldn't. One day you are willing to give up the farm, the pickup, and half the retirement. That's when a good legal advisor will reach through the phone and kick your sorry ass. So, get a good one. Get a referral, interview them, and make sure you click.

13. You will learn how simple it is to file for a divorce.

It's only a matter of filing a set of papers with the court. You get the packet, you fill it out, and take it to an attorney or paralegal. Then you take the papers to the person at the courthouse window; they stamp them and set a court date. You go to court, you settle (in the simplest case), then you file the official papers at the courthouse. In the state of California, you have your divorce six months later.

14. You may also learn how simple it is to rescind your petition for divorce.

If Jim and I were able to work things out, there was a way to stop the divorce from becoming final. Just like filing; you get another form, fill it out, and take it to the person at the window; they stamp it, and you are still married. Knowing this made me feel better about going forward with the divorce proceedings.

HAVING A SOCIAL LIFE WITH CHILDREN

15. You will become familiar with single parent lingo.

"Are you *on* or *off* this weekend?" That's lingo used by divorced people with children. If you have the kids that weekend you are "on." If you don't, you are "off."

The first four years I was divorced, I had my children 80 percent of the time. They were with their father every other weekend, starting Saturday mornings and returning Sunday evenings. There were only two nights a month that I could go on a date or out with friends.

It becomes a timing thing if you want to go out with other divorced friends with children. When your friends switch their schedules, it throws your social calendars off because now you're "off" when they're "on."

16. Your time management skills will improve.

It was hard to suddenly have to play the role of both parents and not have a break for two weeks. When your break does come, it's spent running errands and grocery shopping. If I had a date, I had to make up lost time during the week. Sometimes it meant running to the grocery store on my lunch hour to get a few things.

I could not afford the luxury of talking on the phone for extended periods during the week until after 9 p.m.. Friends and family knew that I would not answer my phone until after 9 o'clock. Between 8:30 and 9:15 I was getting the kids down for bed. If I took a five-minute call, it would set me back thirty minutes. So I learned to unplug the phone and let the message go to my answering machine until I got them to sleep.

As a way to get more time to myself, I trained myself to function on less sleep. To this day I love to stay up late and get up early just to have some quiet alone time. As the children got older, things got easier. Eventually, I was able to leave them home together while I ran a quick errand. In a few years it will get even better, they will be old enough to run errands for me!

17. When you start dating, you will have a curfew.

This is the case if you are court-ordered to pick-up or receive your children by a certain time. It will limit the distance you may travel on your "off" weekends. When I was dating my husband, Todd, he loved to take me camping and hiking, but we always had to be cognizant of the time.

GOING IT ALONE WITH CHILDREN

One of the most painful things about getting divorced was the reality that my children were now from a broken home. More than anything, I felt like my children had been robbed, and there wasn't anything I could do about it. As a parent we want to protect our children at all cost. When your hands are tied and you are helpless to do anything, you just have to have faith that in the end your children will benefit from your strength and determination.

It is sad to think that divorce may happen to them someday, too, and we are their role models. When divorce strikes, we have to play with the hand that is dealt to us. We didn't ask for this, but we can use it as an opportunity to teach our children how to make lemonade out of lemons. In essence, we are teaching them that life doesn't always go according to plan, but when you put your best foot forward, good things will come of it.

As parents we want to protect our children and maintain their innocence for as long as possible. Truth is, divorce is just another fact of life. I was pretty sheltered from it growing up and that was how I wanted it for my children. Instead, they now have three sets of grandparents who love them and an extra parent to protect and guide them through life.

18. Be kind to your ex — at least eventually, and don't talk bad about him in front of the kids.

A friend of mine, Amy, told me that one day her six-year old daughter repeated the story of how daddy met his new girlfriend, Sandra. Amy was driving the car at the time. Her daughter began to repeat the story. She said, "Sandra said she knew when she met daddy that she had to have him." Amy just about slammed on the brakes. After she collected her composure she asked her daughter, "Did Sandra tell you that daddy was *still* married to mommy?"

No matter how cognizant you try to be about not passing judgment on your ex in front of your kids, there are times, when enough is enough and you just have to say something to set the record straight, but remember you are talking about one of their parents. Just because you may not like him or her doesn't mean you should crush your child's image. They will eventually develop their own opinion without your help. Don't teach them to hold your grudges.

My kids love to hear the stories of how their father and I met. It's their history. It doesn't matter to them that our love died, what matters is that it once existed. To them, it pinpoints their beginning. They will ask me about the story of how we met. I embellish the story here and there and try to remember how I once thought of their father. There is always teasing and joking during the story and I remember, they just want to know.

19. When parents fight, the children will have divided loyalty.

Children are gifts from God; they are not to be used as weapons or messengers and they will always defend the underdog parent. They don't care who was right or who was wrong. Just because *you* chose to end the relationship doesn't make it right for you to keep your children from having one. Unless you truly feel the child is in danger, then don't keep them from your ex. If they really don't want to be with their other parent, they will tell you.

And don't make them talk for you. As much as you may detest talking to your ex, do it anyway. Remember, you are setting an example for your children. It is possible they may have to walk in similar shoes someday, too.

20. Be age appropriately honest with your children.

In the beginning I was the bad guy because, to them, it was my fault their dad didn't live with us any more. To them I was the meanie and that's why they didn't get to see their dad. That wasn't it at all. He wouldn't come get them or help me so I could take a break, because it was inconvenient for his new girlfriend and his new lifestyle. But, you can't strike out at a child. You have to put it in their terms, "Daddy doesn't want to play with mommy any more because daddy has a new best friend, and it hurts mommy's feelings." They'd say, "Well maybe if you were nicer to daddy he would want to play with you." It would take everything I had to stop snorting, but I'd compose myself and say, "You will understand someday when you are older."

When children ask about what happened, keep it simple and brief. Children will never understand why their parents couldn't work things out, especially if you become friendly and civil again. They will always hold out hope for a reunion.

21. Live close to your ex, at least while the kids are school age.

Just the other day, my daughter, who is nearly ten years old thus too young to remember when her father and I were married, said to me, "Mom, I wish you and dad were still married." I pried later about why she felt that way and the only reason was because she didn't like living at both houses.

Children don't choose divorce; so it's up to us to see what we can do to make it easier on them? When I asked my children what would have made things easier for them, my son, who was 12 at the time, answered, "It would have been better if you and dad lived closer together."

At first their dad moved on the opposite end of town and because all their activities were in my neighborhood, they were on the road more than they were home, when they were with him. Eventually, both of us moved and we ended up living closer, a fifteen-minute drive apart, and even that was too far for the kids' preference.

It may be hard and you may not like it, but if it's possible, living closer together for the sake of the children will make your life simpler. For one reason or another, it may not be possible. The neighborhood may not be of your choosing, or it may be too far from your job. But if both parents share custody, it will make your life a whole lot simpler as the children get older and you shuttle them between activities and each other.

If your ex lives a long distance away, you will get familiar with the community of divorced people at the airport. You will recognize each other at the airport terminals when you send your kids for a visit with your ex, and you will see them again when you pick up your kids upon their return. Unfortunately, kids in this situation don't get to play on teams and be a part of local activities as much when they are being shuffled between parents and airports this way.

22. Children need stability in their life.

Try to maintain the same schedules between the two households. Keep the routine the same. And if you ever have to move from the house you and their father shared, you will need to explain your reason for moving over and over and over again. They won't understand for a long time.

23. Don't split up their week.

If you share custody, keep it one solid week, one solid weekend. Don't split the week in two. Children need the consistency of weekly household responsibilities, and it gives them more stability to be in one place for a while. My ex and I worked out a situation where I got to see them every morning before school, even when it was his week. He would bring them to me in the morning, and I would get them ready and take them to school. I was the morning person. He was the evening person and picked the kids up from school. So even on my weeks, he got to see the children every day, too. It took away the burden of being a single parent the entire week. More importantly, we were eventually able to work together, and that is the goal.

24. Disciplining children alone is hard.

My parents provided me with solid role models in the discipline department. They were good at it, and they each had back up. I didn't want to make mom mad enough to tell dad, because if dad got wind of it, I was done. My goose was cooked.

As a single parent I had to be both the nurturer and the enforcer. It was a hard role psychologically. I didn't have someone to bounce my anger off of when they misbehaved. As a single parent, I had no back up. I didn't know how hard this would be until one night when I was about to lose it with my son. I called his father for help and intervention. He told me to "Deal with it." It became painfully clear to me that he wasn't going to help me unless he was court ordered and that's how it was for the next four years.

At first, trying to be both mom and dad was tough. I remembered how both my parents tagged teamed and how challenging it was even for the two of them. Dad was the enforcer, the one who did the spanking; mom was the one you didn't want to tick off. I now had the challenge of being both.

I read parenting handbooks, I attended seminars, and I practiced all the psychology I could, but still I lacked something. It's called testosterone. I don't care how you slice it; most teenagers fear their fathers and mock their mothers. I was lucky, eventually I had Todd for support and back up.

Later, by the time my son was a teenager, their father had become more involved in their lives. By this time we shared custody, he did more in the discipline department than he realized, just by being present. The statistics prove this.

Fatherless homes account for 63% of youth suicides, 90% of homeless/runaway children, 85% of children with behavior problems, 71% of high school dropouts, 85% of youths in prison, well over 50% of teen mothers. *(Sources: U.S. Census Bureau, National Center for Health Statistics, Americans for Divorce Reform, Centers for Disease Control and Prevention, Institute for Equality in Marriage, American Association for Single People, Ameristat, Public Agenda)*

For you single moms, don't worry. Male role models are everywhere. I highly recommend year-round sports for teenage boys and girls. Boys and Girls Scouts, part-time jobs with a mentor, and grandparents are also viable alternatives.

25. Always keep in mind that your children come first. This will guide you in your decisions.

It's not about you and your ex anymore. It's about the children. Keeping this in the forefront will help guide you when you are not quite sure what to do. It's not always about *doing* for your kids; it's about doing what's *right* for them. Now that you are a single parent, your life will have challenges you didn't have before. Sure you may be more inconvenienced, now that you have to do it all, but when you weigh the inconveniences out with the benefits, you just learn to suck it up because it will payoff 10-fold in the long run.

Because their father and I had both moved, we were traveling about 24 miles round trip to their schools and daycare each day. Jim got frustrated with the commute because three doors down from his house were neighborhood schools. He pushed for the kids to switch schools. I felt strongly they stay where they were. The school they attended was a "Distinguished" school, which meant it consistently had high scores academically.

Because I had been involved in their activities, I knew all the parents of my children's friends. If I couldn't attend a fieldtrip, it gave me great comfort that I knew at least two or three other parents attending. It takes time to establish history and unless you move out of town there is no need to uproot them from their schools.

After another year of fighting this battle, I caved in and tried to support the change of schools. But, after two months I realized it was the worst post-divorce decision I had ever made. I based the decision on convenience instead of what was best for the kids. Eventually I was able to switch them back, but at first Jim was not happy with me. I struck a deal. I would be the one to drive them to and from school. It was worth it to me.

26. Don't be lazy or selfish with your time or money when it comes to the kids.

What's most annoying to children of divorced parents is the constant keeping of tabs on money and time between the two.

I asked some young adults who came from divorced parents this question: "What advice would you give to parents from a child's point of view?" One twenty-one year old said, "Don't be lazy or selfish with your time or money when it comes to the kids." When I asked him to elaborate he said, "My parents had to split everything to the penny. When it came to doing extra curricular activities, I never could. One was always afraid of getting stuck with the tab. And when it was their weekend to have us we would do nothing but chores. I'd catch pieces of conversations about the fun they had on their outings when they didn't have us the weekend before.

27. Children will give you clarity; they are great teachers of the obvious.

Children can give you immense strength and are great teachers of the obvious, especially when you're caught in a blinding storm. Just asking a child what they want can give you clarity. I'm not talking about leaving decisions up to a child, that's not fair to them. But, when you are confused and need clarity, just ask your child what they think and then just listen, go brain dead after that and don't judge their opinion.

Before Todd and I ever married we had many periods where we didn't see each other. He wasn't ready for a full-time family and was having doubts. I tried very hard to give

him space and sometimes his need for space caused me
great insecurity. One day I was driving with the kids and
we all expressed how we missed him, but I was trying to be
strong and not call. It had been several weeks and I needed
to know he missed me and wanted to come back into my
life. So when my son asked, "Why don't we ever get to see
Todd any more?" I told him because it was too hard for me
to see him right now. This made no sense to an eight year
old. So he says, "If you miss him mom, why don't you just
call him?"

I thought about it for the next three days, until I finally
convinced myself it would be okay to call. Todd was excited
to hear from me and shared how he had been missing us
too. It was one of the many gifts of clarity my children have
given me.

FINANCIAL SET BACKS

28. Divorce is financially devastating, but you will recover.

When my ex left, we were severely in the hole from his
business. I had no choice but to file for bankruptcy. Let me
tell you a thing or two about bankruptcy. You'd better own a
house already and have paid off your car; otherwise, you're
screwed. I had to learn to live on a cash only basis. It is fairly
simple and inexpensive to file for bankruptcy, but I don't
recommend it unless it is your last resort.

29. You will learn how to stretch a dollar.

The first year after a divorce is hard financially, and it
takes effort to get things under control again. I became the
"Serial Slasher." I cut my Internet service and my cable. I
cancelled my cell phone. I gave away our family dog. I had a

garage sale. I even bought a toaster oven just so that I could save energy and not use my big oven.

I found ways to save on my grocery bill, too. McDonalds used to have 39 cent hamburgers every Sunday. Guess who would stock up? I found grocery store outlets to do my marketing, and I looked for farmers markets to buy my produce. My all-time financial low was when I only had $20 to get through the next two weeks, and I had a baby in diapers to boot. I think we ate a lot of Top Ramen and Mac and Cheese those two weeks. My sister invited us to dinner a couple of times, too. I rationed the disposable diapers and used cloth when I was home. I cooked meals in bulk and froze them, I rationed my gas, and we walked or rode bikes for entertainment. As a working mom, I made use of my crock-pot more than ever and I kept my fingers crossed that nothing major broke.

If I wanted to buy something, I usually had to stagger my purchases. I sold my kitchen table and chairs in my garage sale. So when it came time to replace them, I realized I couldn't afford to buy everything in one month. So, the first month I bought the table. The next month I bought one chair. Then next month I bought two more chairs. That's all I really needed. A table and three chairs. For years friends would ask me why I didn't have more chairs. I would tell them the story, and they would tease me about getting another chair.

30. Your survival instinct will kick in, and you will realize you are tougher than you thought. You will find your inner strength and get through it.

If something in the house broke, I learned how to fix it. I got good at installing kitchen faucets and fixing toilets. I learned how to mix and set cement, I refinished a hardwood floor, and laid baseboards. One time a couple of young cable

guys came to install my satellite dish and were going to run
my cable along the outside of my house. I interrupted and
asked that they go under the house. They refused saying they
don't crawl under houses. So I told them to watch and learn.
It must have been amusing to them, but I proceeded to take
the cable and install it myself under the house. Needless to
say they were very impressed and told me I deserved the
'Customer of the Year' award, then we high-fived! You just
do what you have to do.

GETTING REMARRIED

At the time of my divorce, I couldn't even imagine ever
getting remarried. People spoke to me in terms of my
"Someday Man." They told me, "Someday, there will be
another man." It was painfully hard to think about this other
man, but eventually I prayed for him to come, and when he
did, I was convinced he was heaven sent.

The faith I had learned to have as a child and the hope I
learned to carry with me as an adult carried me through the
early months of my divorce. There were days I had lost hope
and during these dark days the expression: "Time heals all
wounds" was the brain numbing thought between my ears.

31. It is hard to give up control of your life again once you have gained it back.

It was funny how set in my ways I became in just a short
period of time. I was able to make all the household decisions and not answer to anyone, except me. When Todd
asked me to marry him, it was an easy decision. What was
hard was giving up some of the control I was used to having.
It's not that I minded giving up control, I was afraid to. It
was just an adjustment I had to make.

32. Your outlook on life will change as well as your perspective on marriage.

After going through hell and back, you do seem to change your perspective on marriage. The second time around, you don't kid yourself about how much work goes into keeping a relationship vital. You know it requires nurturing, and that there will be good and bad times; Most of all, you have a greater appreciation for your spouse.

THE HARDEST PART

The hardest part about getting divorced are the lessons learned getting back to happy. Without a doubt, becoming happy again is the weightlifting regimen of getting back in shape from a divorce. It is a lifestyle change and the focus is on conditioning. What you once knew as normal has been redefined, and you are in the process of redefining yourself and your life. It's the most challenging part of the divorce process, but it will serve you well, and you will be stronger because of it.

In order to start feeling better about myself I first took inventory of my life and looked at the things over which I could control. I started to look at the things in my life that gave me happiness. Then I jotted down a few goals that enabled me to do more of these things. I set goals in increments: monthly, weekly, and daily.

My children gave me the most happiness, but I was always so busy worrying about our dinner and bath schedules that I didn't enjoy them like I should until one fateful day when my best friend tried to coach me out of the blues. She told me to take the kids for a walk. I told her it was raining. After which she told me to put jackets on and get them in a warm bath when we got back, they'd be fine. I still remember that day. We splashed, played, and got soaked in the rain. When we came back they got in the tub, while I started a fire. We sat in front of the fire reading books and playing quietly in our pajamas and we had snacks before dinner.

After that revelation, I decided to scrap the routine more and set one night aside each week for family game night. I decided I wouldn't worry so much about the kids skipping a bath or getting off schedule.

It made me feel secure to have a savings plan and that made me happy. So I set a goal to budget my income. Saving money became contagious, and I would set monthly savings goals. Sometimes it wasn't much, but I paid my mutual funds before everything else and budgeted accordingly. Sometimes all I could afford to save was $25 dollars.

I started to feel alive again when I got to go out with friends. So instead of feeling guilty for not having my children with me, when they were with their dad I went out with friends or did things alone to recharge my batteries. I had fun either way and learned to enjoy being alone.

FROM THE TUELBOX

Mastering the skill of overcoming your circumstances takes time and optimism. You have to realize what you have control over and use your imagination and discipline to change what you can. Sometimes it has to start with changing your outlook. The initial effort will pay off and you'll get your life back. Sometimes finding the happiness within can come from being without.

4

The Crap Meter

WE ALL PUT UP with a certain level of crap in our relationships. Wouldn't it be great if we could put crap on
a scale and give it a standard unit of measure so that when
we talk about how really crappy something is it will be more
relative. We could say, "hey that's a bunch of crap" and it
would be right there in black and white.

People could use the crap meter as a standard for ending
relationships. If you pull a 10 on the meter its an automatic
end to the relationship. You get a 10, you're out! When your
spouse stays out all night and doesn't call, that's a 10! When
your spouse pinches your fat and asks, "Can you pinch an
inch?" that's maybe a 2. It's crap, but you'll put up with it.
When your spouse doesn't notice your new hairstyle, that's
maybe a 4. When your spouse spends money like no body's
business, including yours, that's maybe a 7. And when your
spouse confuses your butt with the tiny blonde's he's just
pinched, that's maybe a 9.

A crap meter is something we all have. For some, it's
instinctual; for others, it's developed over time. Being
in tune with your crap meter is huge because when crap
happens you need to be ready. The saying, "choose your
battles wisely" can be nebulous for someone who has no
scale for their tolerance of crap. It's important to know how
much crap you are willing to put up with in a relationship.

SO WHAT WOULD A CRAP METER LOOK LIKE?

The New Relationship   The Mature Relationship
Crap Meter   Crap Meter

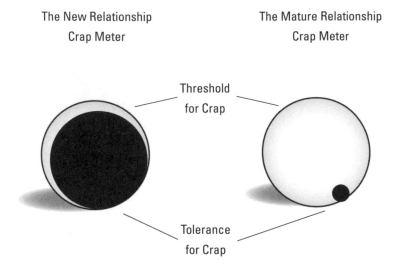

In the diagrams above, the outer circle represents the amount of crap your crap meter can handle – your threshold for crap. The inner circle represents our actual crap meter, it is the amount of crap you are willing to tolerate. At the start of a new relationship, we are willing to tolerate a lot more crap, but as it matures our tolerance levels shrink and so does our crap meter.

Do you see how both diagrams look like eyes? Look for a second and you'll see. The new relationship crap meter has the appearance of surprise, while the mature relationship crap meter looks more like a "beady" eye, watching your every move. See what happens when we put an eyebrow over the crap meter.

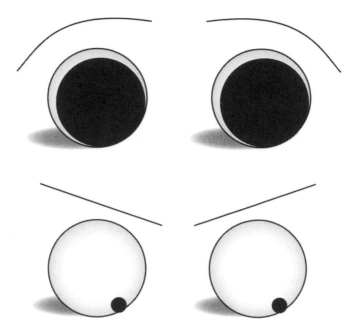

As we get older, we allow less crap into our lives, and nothing surprises us. But when we are younger, when we haven't had a chance to fully engage and develop our crap meter, the things other people try to pull surprise us and may even catch us off guard. We put up with the crap because we don't know yet that we don't have to or because we want to seem accommodating and understanding.

HOW WE LEARN TO DEAL WITH CRAP

There are various types of crap we deal with throughout our lives. There's the type of crap we deal with at work, at home, at school, in our car, and on the streets. There is also relationship crap. New relationship crap deals more with trust and expectations, while Mature crap deals more with respect and consideration. Examples of new and mature relationship crap are as follows:

New relationship crap deals more with trust and expectations... NEW RELATIONSHIP CRAP	Mature relationship crap deals more with respect and consideration... MATURE RELATIONSHIP CRAP
• Not being trusted • Being introduced as a friend • Breaking up over the phone • Same person always pays the tab • Bitchiness • Selfishness • Thoughtlessness • Spending too little thought on special relationship firsts • Expecting your partner to know what you want • Pulling away without warning • Calling too much • Not calling enough • Waiting too late to plan a weekend date • Being late • Not dressing for the occasion • Being too friendly with an ex • Being noncommittal • Canceling a date at the last minute • Not being told that your new lover is married	• Not being respected • Not being heard --having no voice in the relationship • Being undermined • Not having any patience • Not being supportive • Being ridiculed or put down • Lying and cheating • Extended unemployment • Not making the bed • Not cooking or cleaning • Not taking care of expensive possessions • Leaving no gas in the car • Out of control anger • Bouncing checks • Imbalance of household chores • Continual inebriation and driving home drunk • Nagging • No toilet consideration (leaving the seat up, the toilet roll empty) • Having a three-car garage that accommodates everything except a car

Learning to put crap in perspective comes with age. It's not about broadcasting an attitude in your walk or what you choose to wear. You just wake up one day and realize you have choices in life. This comes with maturity and wisdom that only age can bring. And when you figure it out, it is pretty liberating.

We can choose whom we want as friends and whom we want to keep at a distance. Not everyone we trust has our best interests at heart. The older we get, the more issues we bring to our relationships. That's a given and a result of just living. We can chose to keep crap out of our lives and still have a lot of friends.

THE SEVEN CATEGORIES OF PEOPLE

Developing the ability to categorize people is essential if you don't want to deal with their crap. Good or bad, at some level, we all label or categorize others. Once we figure out who fits where, our world spins more smoothly and we have more inner peace. Learning to categorize people also comes with age. When you are younger, you haven't encountered enough people or their issues to know how to categorize them, so you end up putting them in the wrong category and opening yourself up to crap.

It is easier to think in terms of categories when we are trying to classify people. If you have had more than one relationship, then you will know what I am talking about. We do it because it helps us create an initial mental impression and from there we define our initial level of trust. There are hundreds of categories to put people in, but for our discussion we will limit it to seven.

1. Ex Significant Other(s)
2. Family Members
3. Work Peers
4. Social Peers
5. Childhood Friends
6. Professional Relationships (Doctors, plumbers, etc)
7. Other

EX SIGNIFICANT OTHER(S)

We put people with whom we have had significant relationships in this category. That way when we drum up bad
memories from the past we can collectively stereotype them
all.

The great thing about this category is that we don't have
to put up with any more of their crap! Ever!

FAMILY MEMBERS

Family members define where we see ourselves in life.
Our sibling order and the age differences between us and
our brothers and sisters also helps categorize peers in our
siblings' age groups and to some degree how we relate to
them.

Family Crap is something we just have to learn to deal
with; there is really no avoiding it. The best way to keep the
family crap at a distance is not to meddle or offer an opinion.
By not taking the bait and engaging in the conversation, you
reserve your opinion. It is very difficult for someone to draw
you into a conversation when they don't know where you
stand. And let's face it, family conversations between siblings
are all about taking sides.

WORK PEERS

We relate to people at work in the same way we did on
the playground. To a large extent our childhood friends and
schoolmates can be found in the faces of our co-workers.
There's the teacher's pet, the nerds, the friends we pass
notes to and tell secrets with, the ones that won't share, and
the ones we want on our team.

SOCIAL PEERS

These are our good friends and the people with whom we like to spend time. We have a lot in common with them. They are the folks we have known forever, and some we have just met.

CHILDHOOD FRIENDS

These are the people we have known all our lives. Because they are like family and we share a common history, we accept them for who they are. People who don't have that history might not understand them the way we do or accept their idiosyncrasies. We are more tolerant of their life choices.

PROFESSIONAL RELATIONSHIPS

When we have to deal with professionals for services we need, invariably we are subjected to some kind of crap. At some level, we even expect it, but not the moment we pick up the phone to set the appointment. All we wanted was a real person and we get an IVR (interactive voice response) system. Is it just me or is it crap when you press "0" to get a live attendant, but instead it takes you to another recorded menu. Everyone knows "0" is the universal number for live attendant. What's with these companies that try to trick us? You can almost hear them developing the system: "Okay, so when they try to outsmart us with the zero routine, let's send them to our two minute survey."

I also think it is crap when the phone or cable company gives you an eight hour window for an appointment, but that's just me. I'm silly I guess.

OTHER

This is the catch-all category for people we meet but with whom we wouldn't necessarily socialize or even call on the phone. They are acquaintances.

WHAT WE CATCH CRAP FOR

We get crap from our significant others for our actions: for talking, breathing, looking, eating, sleeping, drinking – sometimes just for being alive. If it can be done, we can catch crap for it. Heck, we even catch crap for the things we fail to do.

HOW OTHERS TEACH US ABOUT
THEIR CRAP METERS

Others teach us about their crap meters with verbal retaliation. Comments when you are driving like, "Did you get a good enough look at those tits on legs? You certainly stared at them long enough! My god, you almost got us killed. Hope it was worth it, dear!" This sends the message, loud and clear, that taking your eyes off the road to stare at well-endowed women will get a verbal retaliation and possibly a physical one.

Others teach us their tolerances for crap with instant physical retaliation. This would be the drink in the face, the slamming door hitting your posterior, the coffee cup against the wall, even the silent treatment.

A CRAP METER IS LIKE A PARKING METER

A red flag means your time has expired or you've committed a violation; soon the meter maid will be by to give you a ticket. When the meter maid is your spouse you can try to act innocent, but don't. Either make an apology or kiss your sex life good-bye. Too many tickets will end your driving privileges and a warrant will be issued. Instead of going to court (where your spouse is the judge, jury, and executioner), it's better to just pay the fines than give excuses because the meter maid doesn't care.

HAVING A CLEARLY DEFINED CRAP METER

If we want to teach others what tilts our crap meter, then we better be in tune with what really ticks us off and what we are and are not willing to put up with in a relationship. Usually our past relationships define this for us. For example:

- If you were ignored in your last relationship, you won't tolerate anything less than being number one.
- If you were cheated on, you won't tolerate flirting.
- If you were hurt financially, you won't tolerate poor money management skills.
- If your last partner was on disability your entire relationship (but managed to play golf every week), then you won't tolerate unemployment.
- If your last relationship ended because of drinking, you won't tolerate hanging out at bars.

33. Things that didn't work in your last relationship will be magnified on your crap meter.

It is a good rule of thumb to find out what ended your partner's last relationship. There are huge clues in their answer. If he says, "it ended because of her poor money management skills," then it probably isn't a good idea to let him know you have a credit card from every major department store.

Also, be very clear about where you stand on all your crap meter issues at all times. For example:

34. Never marry a man whose bar tab has to be rolled into a refi.

Know how much financial crap you are willing to handle. If you need to save $10,000 for a new roof and your partner wants to spend his Friday paycheck at the local pub getting liquored up, then that's crap.

When your crap meter tilts, follow through and stand your ground. If it is something that is truly important to you, say so. But not everything is a deal breaker. Pick and choose your battles wisely, and when you do, take a stand. Stay strong. The hard work will pay off for you and your relationship later.

I remember a financial battle with my current husband. We had just leased a brand new Volvo, and five months later Todd switched careers and needed a truck instead. He knew we would take it in the shorts if we traded in the Volvo, so he wanted to trade in my three-year-old Explorer that was paid for and comfortably sat the entire family and then some. It was hard, but I stood my ground and wouldn't let him do it. I liked the Volvo, but we couldn't afford it all. The Volvo and his BMW motorcycle had to go if he wanted a new truck. It took a good week to reach an agreement, but he got his truck and I got to keep the Explorer, and neither of us felt resentful.

Understanding how to reach a good compromise brought us closer together because we learned we could handle conflict in the marriage. The rule of thumb about compromises in marriage is simple: When neither of you gets everything you want, it's a good compromise.

FINE TUNING YOUR CRAP METER

Crap happens in an instant. We seldom see it coming and can be broadsided on impact. Fine tuning your crap meter takes no time at all. It's as simple as having a sense of what's right and what's wrong something we usually know by the time we are four. So why do so many suffer so long without a finely turned crap meter?

Putting the crap meter into practice is not easy because it means you have to be confrontational. So many people would rather bury their heads in the sand and hope the crap goes away. They don't even recognize crap because they are too busy walking the eggshell tightrope their spouses or others have so graciously built for them. Their focus isn't on fair treatment anymore; it's on survival.

It's easy to get your point across in extreme cases of crap. Even the most passive person will shout "foul play" when their life is in jeopardy. But in the less extreme cases of crap it isn't always easy to stay consistent. I'm talking about the kind of crap that is subtle and comes in cycles, the kind of crap that catches you off guard and is from the people you care about the most. You have to consciously remind yourself about that kind of crap.

For years, my friend, Jackie, had a jogging partner, Kelly. Everyday they would run together on their lunch hour. Jackie confided in me that running with Kelly used to be a lot of fun and was their time to share. But over the years, she said Kelly started to change and their exchanges were more contrite. Whenever Jackie shared news with Kelly, Kelly would have an opinion or make some judgment about Jackie. Jackie decided it took more emotional than physical energy to complete the run. She didn't want to hurt Kelly, but Kelly was hurting her and didn't seem to care.

I asked Jackie, "Why don't you tell her she is upsetting you?" Jackie replied, " For years I have tried to point out how she is condescending and doesn't treat me as her equal, and it never changes. I used to care and value the friendship enough to talk to her about it, but now I know it will change for about three weeks and then start all over again. It's a bunch of crap!"

It happens in all kinds of relationships: romantic, platonic, or otherwise. We simply get to a point of indifference and stop valuing the friendship. To preserve yourself and not feel badly about pulling away, you need to change how you categorize the person. Someone who used to hold a high rank in your life as a social peer now must be reclassified as an "Other" to avoid any further hostility. Once you realize you cannot change a person, you have two choices: Either accept them as they are or teach them that you have a finely tuned crap meter and you are not afraid to use it.

The beauty about the crap meter is that you can teach others about your tolerances without saying anything. I advised Jackie to change her routine and run alone and not to talk to Kelly for awhile.

In cases of extreme crap we are more apt to speak up, but in cases of subtle and more consistent crap, we should just reclassify these people in our lives and temporarily change our behavior toward them.

A finely tuned crap meter will eliminate a lot of negativity in your life. Once she stopped running with Kelly, Jackie said she started to feel better about herself and her thoughts were more positive. She started saying "Hi" to people Kelly had problems with and was able to decide for herself if they were actually good people.

CRAP METER ENVY

Crap Meter envy, also known as being a wuss, is when you know something is crap and you sit there and take it. You take it because you don't know how not to. You envy those people who can speak their minds and don't care about whose feelings they hurt. You want a crap meter, but you just haven't got what it takes. Don't get caught with crap meter envy.

The way to avoid crap meter envy is to develop an attitude and keep one thought in mind: "To hell with you!" After that you simply go brain dead and let the forces of nature take over. There's no analyzing involved. Why worry about hurting the feelings of someone who is being disrespectful to you? Internalizing this attitude and keeping it bottled up inside does you no good.

Physical force is not necessary to overcome crap meter envy. All it requires is a sense of self worth and a mouth. Let me show you what I mean.

IF AUNT JEMIMA HAD A CRAP METER

Aunt Jemima is an American icon we all know as the warm loving face on the syrup bottle who sweetens our pancakes. We think of her as a loving jovial woman from the South that whips up the best breakfast for miles and takes pure delight in doing so. But what if Aunt Jemima had a crap meter, which included no patience for laziness or disrespect. What if you heard her say, "Get off your lazy behind and churn me some butter fool!" Yes, it's hard to imagine Aunt Jemima with a short fuse. But I bet she didn't raise any lazy children or put up with crap from her husband.

CALIBRATING YOUR CRAP METER

There are rules of engagement to remember when calibrating your crap meter. Don't mull it over in your mind until you can think of a polite way to challenge the crap. It's crap, so call a spade a spade and engage. Shout "bullshit"

from the top of your lungs. Now you've got it. You just calibrated your Crap Meter.

Rules of Engagement:

1. Don't hold back.
2. Develop a "too bad, too sad" attitude
3. Be consistent
4. Be prepared for round 2
5. Stand your ground and don't back down
6. Draw your line
7. Know your "why" (Why you are picking this battle)

35. After you have gone through a divorce, your crap meter gets more acutely tuned.

Divorce does that for you. It jump starts the crap meter
calibration process. You will look back on all the crap you
put up with in your marriage and ask yourself, why did I
allow that for so long? After you realize how big a wuss you
were, to tolerate the crap you endured, you in essence calibrate your meter for crap. This process of pondering the
past, realizing how you were sucked in, and then liberating
yourself with a new found attitude is all part of calibrating
your crap meter.

My friend Mark went through a divorce and later discovered that his wife had been embezzling money from his
business account. Not only did Mark get spanked with this
discovery, but he had to pay her alimony. After his lesson, he
became very intolerant of women who just wanted his money.
He was tired of dating women who expected him to pay all
the time after they found out how much he was worth. Mark
got to be an expert at restaurant bill paying body language.
He was happy to pay the bill for a woman who made eye
contact with him when the check came, or who even offered
to pay her half, but his crap meter would tilt when there was

an expectation that he pay the bill without even a gracious "thank you."

THREATENING THE MARRIAGE
AS YOUR TRUMP CARD

The words, "I want a divorce" should never be uttered in a good marriage. You might allow a one-time slip up, but anything more than that is crap! Hearing your spouse threaten to end the marriage is very scary the first time you hear it. But the second and third time, you finally realize this is a false trump card. When a spouse uses that trump card in the heat of a marital spat, pull out your Ace and call the bluff. Someone who uses the marriage in this way is very controlling. Take the control away and issue a challenge. Chances are your spouse did not really mean it and will not follow through. Spouses that threaten to end the marriage are either too ignorant or evil, or just don't know an intelligent way to ask for a compromise. If your spouse is like this, run and run fast!

EVERY NOW AND THEN STUPID COMES OVER

Have you ever met Stupid at your doorstep? Stupid has no concept of time and that's why Stupid shows up at dawn. Stupid's bad memory and lack of accountability in the relationship might explain why Stupid can't retain numbers, least of all Stupid's own phone number. Stupid gets confused easily, so it is only natural that the first thing out of Stupid's mouth when Stupid greets you is, "What?" Stupid forgets Stupid isn't really a doctor, but that doesn't stop Stupid from being fascinated with your health. Stupid insists on knowing what all your problems are right now. Stupid will ask, "What's your problem?"

When Stupid comes over you should quickly whip out your crap meter, calibrate it a time or two and then let Stupid have it!

The way to deal with Stupid is with the vacuum cleaner. If Stupid kept you up all night worrying and wondering where he was, when Stupid finally comes home at 7 in the morning thinking he's going to lay down and sleep, you just tell him, "No way!" When he hits the rack anyway, that's when you get busy. You don't need to say another word; just go to your broom closet and pull out Old Electric Betsy. Get her ready and start her engine. Stupid will close the bedroom door next. Don't let that stop you. In fact, that's almost better. Just let Old Betsy run outside the door. Have you ever heard the sound of an idling vacuum cleaner? In about two minutes, Stupid will be out of the house for the rest of the afternoon.

36. You will learn how to say, "no" to the opposite sex.

You will feel a little overwhelmed with your new life situation (especially if you are the sole caregiver and provider for your children) and your tolerance for anyone who tries to screw up what you've worked so hard for will be nil.

THE MOM AND DAD STORY (MATURE CRAP)

After spending the entire weekend with my parents, I watched as they bickered back and forth and irritated each other all day. I asked myself, how can two people who have loved each other since they were sixteen drive each other crazy then within seconds be over the drama and onto the next subject and at the end of the day still curl up with each other on the couch for a movie? The kicker is they didn't even think they had bickered or argued at all that day. At 67, my parents are too young to be senile, but I had to wonder how they could feel this way after what I witnessed. Did they just forget how they drove each other nuts? At the end of the day, did it all just get wiped from the memories? How awesome a trait is that!

I think because they've been together for so long, they can only put up with each other's crap for about two seconds before they have to say something. Holding their tongues after all these years isn't in their relationship make-up.

After spending nearly 49 years together in holy matrimony they know what buttons to push and they push them hard and they push them often. It works for them. I asked my mom how they do it. She replied, "We both just have really small crap meters, I guess. We don't put up with much from each other any more." Amen, brother!

It works for them because they learned early how not to hold a grudge. They learned at a young age to speak their minds. As they got older, they realized why that is so important. According to my mother, "When you can speak your mind and not worry about hurting the other person's feelings, you are free to disagree." In other words, when you don't have to worry about sugar coating everything you say, you can let the other person know how you feel. You can say it, get it off your chest, and move on. Another term for this is "Justified Nagging." My parents don't pick their battles anymore. Everything is pretty much fair game. Because they have fine-tuned their crap meters with each other over the years, they know before they act how the other one will react. There are no guesses and no unknowns. That is the beauty of how a finely turned crap meter can work.

My parents are ying and yang personified. They have been together so long that they both know where each other's meters will register depending on the circumstance. For example, my dad will say, "Your mother's gonna shit when she finds out Mr. Cross is stirring up dust in his pasture again. I better go close the doors," or, "You better not tell your mom how much I paid for this old car part, she'll make me sell one of my other cars for sure." My mom is the same. She'll say, "Don't tell your dad what I paid for this bracelet; he'll have to sell one of his cars."

FROM THE TUELBOX

The lesson to be learned is to be on guard and shield yourself from crap. This is accomplished by gauging your spouse's crap meter. Your spouse's crap meter is something to behold and respect. Our marriage vows taken a step further could almost include a line about it – "to love honor and cherish each other's crap meters". It is not something to be ignored. Calibrating your crap meter wisely and being in tune to your spouse's will aid the life expectancy of any marriage.

The School of Hard Knocks has a Drama Department for Divorcees with Crap Meter issues. Every divorcee must enroll in a semester of acting. This is for your own good. Courses offered include:

- **Appreciation of Acting** (how to act like you care)
- **Modern Drama** (how to appreciate not having any)
- **Principles of Choreography*** (how to dance your way out of any accusation)
- **Voice and Movement*** (how not to make a smart mouth comment as you make your grand exit)

*Course is primarily for non-majors.

5

Betrayal: Surviving An Affair

WHEN YOU ARE THE victim of an affair, the only way to survive that first year is to develop a sense of humor and have a lot of support. Be vengeful, but only in your mind. Right or wrong, it helps. There is humor in everything; You just have to find it - even if it kills you. Here's something to start you off. If your spouse left you for someone else know this, marriage results from an affair less than 9% of the time and the divorce rate for such marriages is 70%.

THE LARONDA TAX

I worked for a tax agency for 12 years, part of the time as a legislative specialist. My job was to review how proposed legislation would impact the state's revenue department. Some of the proposed taxes and credits were almost comical; we would affectionately name them as they moved through the legislature. After my divorce, I came up with what I called the "LaRonda Tax," affectionately named after my husband's mistress. When this woman made picking up the pieces of my life difficult, I tried to find ways to get silent retribution. I figured if my ex was going to be stupid then he should be taxed accordingly.

So, I filed for child support. I affectionately referred to my child support payments as the LaRonda Tax. It made coping with raising two small children on my own easier.

Child support is actually better than a tax. It's a double whammy. The person who pays child support has to pay taxes on that income, whammy number one. And, the person who receives the payment does not have to include it as income whatsoever. It is money free and clear on the receiver's end, whammy number two.

37. You will experience joy again.

Especially on your way to the bank to deposit that first child support check, and then again when you have a new set of boobs financed by those checks. For the guys out there, I'm only sort of kidding. Men that are raising children on their own, juggling a career and life with kids can find joy in knowing by taking care of business you are taking control. You will find joy in knowing that your efforts will prevent the abuse of the child support checks...

I'm not quite sure why, but after their speedy marriage LaRonda took it upon herself to write out the child support check each month. I guess she wanted to make sure that I knew she took his name. Contrary to her intention, it made me feel even better about calling it the LaRonda Tax. Although I could afford my own hair appointments, manicures, etc. I would pretend that she was the source of the funds for all of my self-indulgences. Not that there were many indulgences, nor was my child support that extravagant, but if I believed she was paying for it, it made whatever the indulgence that much sweeter. Don't get me wrong, the money was by no means abused; I had a career that could support us. It was just my own way of evening up the score.

COPING WITH THE INITIAL SHOCK

The Blah-blam! Either you see divorce coming and deny it, or you don't see it coming at all. I saw it coming for a few years, but I couldn't find a way to make things better. We had stopped laughing. There was little fun left in the marriage, but in my heart I really wanted things to change. It is a very helpless feeling when you are at the stage where you want to make things better, but can't. There is a sense of despair that comes over you. Talking about it only seems to make it worse, so you worry, a lot or just adapt to being unhappy. You start noticing how happy everyone else is. Yet, you stay together, hoping things will change. Then Blah-blam! You know the Blah-blam I'm talking about.

Fay, a young radiology technician, described her Blah-blam to me this way. One morning, she was at the grocery store, thinking she had this happy little life. Then, when she returned home, she found her spouse cheating on her with another woman in her own bed. **Blah-blam!**

Keith, a hardware store owner came home from work one day to find the only thing waiting for him was a ton of bills and a note from his spouse that read, "I'm out of here and I left with your best friend, Steve. Cook your own dinner!" **Blah-blam!**

My Blah-blam came the night Jim confessed to seeing another woman. I was devastated. Getting news that our marriage was over before it was legally over was the hardest thing to grasp – until I got a handle on reality. Reality like hearing their names mentioned together, seeing him act differently towards me, seeing his physical appearance change (shedding the weight), seeing him happy when I was nothing but sad, knowing he didn't care about my well-being or whether I was dead or alive, or knowing that anything he did for me was only out of guilt or obligation. Those little doses of reality sting, but it's better to stand before the firing squad and take all your hits at once. I had to believe the man upstairs had a better plan for me.

THE S.I.C.K. PRINCIPLE

The process by which you realize your loved one is having an affair is what I call the S.I.C.K. principle. S.I.C.K. is an acronym for the steps we go through before we are convinced. S.I.C.K. stands for:

Suspect

Investigate

Confirm

Kick Ass

During this time, we literally feel sick. I liken it to a hybrid between feeling nauseous and stressed out. It's a combination of the panic we feel when we see cop lights flashing in our rear view mirror and the pure shock after witnessing a fatal car accident. It's in that same family of emotions as shock and panic. It's that sinking moment when we say, "Oh My God!" This is what it is like to realize our spouse is having an affair.

SUSPECT

The first part of the discovery is suspecting that something isn't right. We suspect our spouse is up to something and it isn't good. We start to question everything they do. We notice little things about their behavior that are out of the norm. Things they say or do don't add up. So we start to check out their story and follow our gut instinct. Everyone has a gut instinct, but many people choose to ignore it. We dismiss it, thinking we are being foolish and even feel a little guilty for being so mistrusting of our partner. But don't. I follow the Ronald Reagan philosophy on enemy trust: "Trust but verify." Trust what your spouse says; then quietly verify it. The first time I suspected something was up and couldn't verify his story was the first time I felt that sick feeling.

I remember people asking me how I knew my husband was having an affair. At the time I wasn't sure why he was acting so funny; I just knew something was up. It was unlike him to be on the phone at weird times and then hang up as soon as I walked into the room. It was more than that though; As anyone who has been the victim of an affair will agree - it is just a gut feeling you have, and you know.

38. Your ex will suddenly become concerned about his looks and smells.

My ex was always a blue jeans and tennis shoes guy. His idea of getting ready for work was rolling out of bed and tossing his hair in a ball cap. My eyebrow lifted when I noticed he was wearing aftershave to work and fussing more in the bathroom.

Every man or woman knows the signs of betrayal, whether or not we acknowledge it. It is the little inconsiderate things they start to do, the unspoken gestures, the impatient behavior, the need to be critical, etc. At some point you start to question yourself. Then when you realize you didn't do anything to provoke the moodiness, you begin to examine other causes. In my case, I began to ask my friends who worked with him.

We know something is wrong, and we are sick about it. During this time, they won't communicate with us, and instead, they treat us like shit. When we just can't take it any more, we muster the courage to ask them to leave. We need space just to calm our nerves.

INVESTIGATE

Just suspecting that something is awry isn't enough for most of us to risk confronting our spouse. We don't want to be wrong if we are going to accuse them of having an affair. There is nothing worse than not trusting someone who is innocent. Naturally, we want to trust our spouse, and when we become suspicious, we feel guilty and doubt ourselves. We don't want to believe what we are feeling or to suspect such dishonesty. So we convince ourselves that we have the problems instead, and we sit and wait for more signs.

Everyone knows the statistics on infidelity, yet we are astonished when it hits home. Why wouldn't we be? Most people don't expect to find out their trusted partner has been sneaking around with the housekeeper, the gardener, the neighbor or someone else when they're off at the grocery store. Most people never see it coming. And there are many reasons for that. By this time, the relationship is on auto-pilot, and we're thinking everything is hunky dory.

For those of us who miss the warning signs, we require more drastic proof. We are blind or in denial and require the frying pan treatment. If you have ever watched Popeye cartoons, you know what I'm talking about. We need to get smacked upside the head a few more times with the frying pan before we see the writing on the wall. In the cartoons, the frying pan left the cartoon character's face flattened like a pancake. But that's okay – eventually we'll see it coming and duck.

After I found out that I had been betrayed, I played the last two years of my life in reverse. The reels would spin; then I'd make a realization. Like the editor of my own crime story, I would say, "Hold it! Play that one again, Johnny." I would play it out again in my head, this time searching for more clues.

Wouldn't it be nice if we had a way of exposing all the signs of a cheating spouse? So many times and in so many ways, cheaters can cover their trail, with no trace evidence of the affair to be found. In this high-tech age, everything is either done with passwords or can be deleted. Until the invention of Luminal, murderers used to be able to cover their trail. Forensic scientists use Luminal at crime scenes to illuminate blood residue. Simply cleaning up the blood isn't good enough anymore. You can pristinely clean the room such that the naked eye would never know blood was shed there. It is truly shocking to see Luminal at work. Suddenly, when viewed under the ultra violet light, you are submerged in the blood bath of the murderous scene. Too bad there isn't Luminal for a cheating spouse. For each cheating phone call, for each time they leave for an errand, for each time they disappear, blood doesn't spill, but the innocent spouse, the victim, loses just a little bit of his or her life. Luminal for a cheater would reveal the evidence of a shattering heart.

This is about the time the crying starts.

CONFIRM – THE NEED TO KNOW

Most people don't ask for a divorce just because they suspect something. People need 100 percent certainty and cold, hard facts before they take action.

When I worked for a tax agency, we were required to abide by certain disclosure rules. One called the "Need to Know" principle worked like this. Just by virtue of working for the agency, you had a "*Right* to Know" confidential tax information to perform your duties. But, not everyone has the "*Need* to Know." You violated disclosure rules if you did not have a *need* to know and were caught browsing confidential information. The punishment was severe fines and jail time.

Like the tax disclosure rule, spouses have both the *right* and the *need* to know what's going on. That's their prerogative by virtue of marriage.

By the time you begin to suspect something is wrong, chances are the affair is in full swing. You crave confirmation and start asking questions. This is when we do crazy things to get our answers. We cross the line a lot during this stage. We assume identities, go undercover, snoop, and make up outlandish lies, checking some of our integrity at the door. People who have never been through something like this don't understand how powerful the *need* to know is. You have the *right* to know if your partner is cheating and you *need* to know without a doubt to exercise your right to file for a divorce.

I remember holding out hope that he hadn't slept with her. In my mind, once he admitted to me that he had slept with her, the marriage would end. It would be my green light to file for a divorce. It is funny how we have these boundaries. I suppose if he had been out of the house for an entire year and told me nothing was going on I would have believed it and held out hope. All the while I would be cheating myself by being so naive. The bottom line is: we need hard cold evidence before we feel right about filing for a divorce. Nobody files for a divorce based on suspicions. By the time someone files, he or she has a confession or all the cold, hard evidence needed. There is no guessing.

Even if you are a pretty stable person by nature, not having confirmation can make you insanely insecure until you get some answers. If something is gnawing at you, it's probably your gut. Listen to it. Find out if something is going on or not. Make some phone calls or pay some visits to places or people that can give you answers, but don't compromise your integrity—well, at least not too much.

When Jim left, he left me with our twenty-two month old daughter and our five-year old son. My daughter still was not sleeping all through the night. One night in particular she woke up hungry. After I fed her I could not settle my mind. I still didn't have my confirmation and it was driving me crazy. So I called him on the phone at 3:30 in the morning. My call went unanswered and it was as if someone socked me in the gut. A friend had given me the address of the woman I suspected he was with that night. So I paid her a visit at 4:30 a.m. My goal was to catch him with her and get my confirmation.

So like a trooper I bundled up my two children and we made the thirty-minute drive. I got lost, but I was determined to get my answer. I finally found her apartment and awoke my children. His truck was nowhere to be found and I almost left the scene, but I had come this far and had to get my answer. As I carried my daughter in one arm and held the hand of my son in the other, we made our way up the flight of stairs to her apartment. I did the unthinkable and knocked. She came to the door and studied me at first, then she said something odd. She said, "You cut your hair." I didn't know she knew what I looked like. I asked if Jim was there. She explained he had left just a short while before. Then she invited us in. It was my chance to plead my case. So without hesitation I said, "I still love my husband and these are his two children." She wasn't sure what to make of me. She said they had some drinks and that was it. She told me she wouldn't get involved until he was divorced. I was dumbfounded, so I got up to leave and calmly reminded her who I was and how I loved him." It was all the confirmation I needed.

KICK ASS - THE CONFRONTATION

Once we have confirmation, we want to kick some ass. We've just realized we have been betrayed by someone we love, and that hurts. What you do next will either make or break you. Here's how to kick ass without resorting to physical violence.

The confrontation is one of those defining moments in our relationship and our life. It is something we will remember for a long time and tell fellow betrayees. It is something we will pass down from generation to generation.

So be wise. Make it classy, make it memorable, and make it law abiding. This section will tell you how to do all that and give your spouse the boot without ever actually getting your shoes dirty.

39. Rule of thumb: don't believe anything the cheater tells you during this phase. Unless he/she makes a confession, don't believe it. They have nothing to gain by the truth.

To start, why not just ask your partner if there is something going on? The goal of the confrontation is to get a confession. If we simply ask, we run the risk of having our suspicions dismissed by our cheating partners, and we get nowhere.

In all likelihood, if we ask, they won't tell. Why should they? They've got the best of both worlds. That's why you need hard evidence when you confront them. Your chances of a confession are much greater if you catch them with the smoking gun.

At this stage, you want them to know that you know and the jig is up! It's important for you to get the jump on the dump. You see, the cheater might be tired of living a lie and almost want to get caught; or maybe he or she doesn't want to hurt you. If you ambush them with evidence and facts, they will be surprised at your brilliance. The cheater is pretty smug in thinking he/she is smarter than you, by hiding it from you. When you pull anchor on their cruise ship, it's like sinking the Titanic.

When I confronted Jim the next day about my 4:30 a.m. visit he acted indignant. Unlike the first time I questioned him about her, he did not deny it this time.

As victims, we want to discuss the affair, so we can work on the marriage. But don't, not yet. There's no discussing the matter with the cheater, at least not at this time. If you do, you will give up your control. You see, cheaters blame us for the affair. It's twisted, I know, but that is how they think. We are the reason for their unhappiness, for the lack of passion in the bedroom. It is our fault they don't love us anymore; We drove them away. That's when we say, "BULLSHIT!" and calibrate our crap meter once and for all.

Jeannie's husband eventually left her for her good friend and neighbor. When Jeannie looked back on the past 18 years of their relationship, she gave countless examples of how she accommodated his "flavor of the month" interests. When he wanted to quit his job to be his own boss, she supported him and worked harder to get a promotion at her job. When he wanted to buy a boat, she said okay, even though he played (and drank heavily) on it every weekend. When he wanted to buy a camper, she went along, even though camping with a toddler was not her thing. When he wanted to buy an expensive bike, she agreed, even though he rode much too fast for her and her daughter. All the while, he wasn't working full-time and barely made enough to cover the mortgage. Jeannie put it this way, "I thought some of that selfishness would go away after our daughter was born, but it never did. It just became a moving target that I could never hit, until eventually he did the ultimate selfish act and betrayed me."

The following table gives you better insight into the cheater. You may recognize some of the traits. Cheaters want the best of both worlds and will try to make their partners feel insecure, jealous and needy.

THE CHEATER/VICTIM PROFILE

Profile of the Cheater

- Spoiled – needs to have the best of everything
- Inconsistency with jobs
- Addictive behavior
- Misguided principles and morals
- Insecure
- Non-confrontational
- Non-communicator
- Disrespecting
- Lives in the here and now
- Self-centered
- Have never been cheated on

Profile of the Victim

- Steady as a Rock
- Holds it together
- Supporter (financially, emotionally, socially)
- Consistent
- Committed
- Determined
- Survivor
- Futuristic
- Not self-centered
- Sacrificing
- Pleaser

Cheaters are often confused and will hold off disclosing anything until they decide what they want to do about the affair. It's very narcissistic.

40. There is nothing like the lynch mob that will come to your aid when you've been cheated on.

It's no big revelation, but the general public considers people who cheat on their spouse despicable. It's not only foolish to fool around with a married person, but nothing gets friends and family more fired up than a cheating spouse. The entire La Famillia of the innocent spouse will be after them. It is a small world and word gets around fast.

The good thing about being the victim of an affair is that everyone sides with you. Right or wrong, they do. My husband and I used to have the same hairstylist, Johnnie. He and his gay lover worked side by side in their shop. Johnnie was so mad at my husband he couldn't wait to see him for his next haircut. My husband had a full head of hair, but Johnnie said he was going to suddenly discover a bald spot.

It never actually happened, but it was good for a laugh. My husband had the sense to not only abandon me, but also our family and friends, including Johnnie.

GET A JUMP ON THE DUMP

The last thing the cheater expects is for us to be strong. They want to lash out at us. It will hurt, but remember the affair is not your fault. The respectable thing for two married people to do is try and work on the marriage together. I remember my husband telling me he tried. I must have been in a coma, because I never knew he was that unhappy or that he was trying to work out any marital problem. How can you work things out if you aren't told about the problem? It wasn't fair for him to say that. His idea of working on it was cheating on me and seeing someone else. That was his way of "trying" I suppose.

Many victims of betrayal falsely blame the affair for the failure of their marriage or relationship. That is only half right. Something is usually missing in the relationship for your partner to have had an affair in the first place. Having an affair is wrong, plain and simple, and people who have them have a huge character flaw, no doubt. But we have to look beyond that if we are to ever heal.

If someone had told me infidelity is symptomatic of an unhappy marriage when I was going through my anger stage, I would have said, "that is such bullshit." Truth be known, we did have problems, and who doesn't? But you can't fix them alone or with an affair.

Every marriage starts out with 110% of best intensions. My marriage to Jim was no exception. In the beginning, it was easy to be around him. He had a kind soul. I think Jim just wanted somebody to settle down with and live a simple life. That was what I wanted too, but after I finished my Master's degree and started my career. I was too unsettled and had too many dreams and aspirations for Jim's liking. By not sharing the same dreams, we made "settling down" not so simple for each other. He wanted a business and I didn't, and when it failed, he lost himself and I became resentful of the debt. Our marriage was missing a deep soul connection, I can't say that it ever had it, but what I mistakenly thought we did have was commitment.

No one deserves to be the victim of an affair and nothing in life can prepare you for it. There are ways of ending a marriage without betrayal of this magnitude. Let the marriage end legally first. It was beyond me at the time how my spouse could have been interested in someone else. I still loved my husband and couldn't even think about dating, let alone sleep with, someone else. But that's the mindset of the one dumped. We are months behind in the recovery process, because we were uninformed and clueless.

If it is any comfort, they have stuffed their feelings for us down deep, but they will surface eventually. Just be patient. On the flip side, *our* emotions are ever present. We are dealing with the gamut of emotions from complete and utter sadness to extreme anger to numbness. For this reason alone, we will heal exponentially faster than they will.

Once we get confirmation, it is important to ask ourselves two questions.

The First Question: "Am I willing to live without trust?" Understand that, if you remain in the marriage, this will last a long time.

The Second Question: "Can my spouse handle all my suspicious questions until I can trust again?"

Asking these questions will give us a better understanding of our crap meter for betrayal, whether we can live with it or not. Our crap meter is our guide for what we are willing to tolerate. Now, more than ever, it's time to fine tune it.

THE OUCH FACTOR

During the first weeks of the initial separation, you feel powerless. Your spouse has left, and all you can think about is them being with another person. You can't sleep at night because this vision gnaws at you.

When you are betrayed by someone it puts the break up on a whole new level. The confusion you feel about "why" is like trying to figure out what is beyond the stars. It's staggering and when you try to figure it out, you just end up back at square one begging the question –why? You just have to have faith that this is all part of a bigger plan – that something better is in store for you. Without this kind of optimism you can get stuck. And if letting it go is too hard at first, start with letting it go for just five minutes at a time.

41. Get wicked — it'll make you feel better.

Eventually you are going to have to snap out of it. Don't keep being a pushover and stop being be so damn nice to someone who has left you holding the bag. This is how big of a chump I was. I folded his clothes neatly, boxed them up and set them under the carport until he was ready to come get them. Most women would have thrown his stuff on the lawn, turned on the sprinklers and said, "Come get your shit, now asshole!" **Ouch!**

42. Get a "F--Off" Attitude

After my initial shock, I decided to get a *F—Off* attitude. I got mad and then I got better. I was tired of playing the poor victim. The amazing thing is, once I changed my attitude, I got stronger. The F—Off attitude is a mindset that places you in the driver's seat to play a little reverse psychology on your spouse.

The first slap of reality for the cheater spouse is when they call or come by the house and there are changes. **Ouch!** I highly recommend making them as soon as possible. The first is your voice mail message. Your spouse no longer lives there; it's your house. This will get a reaction.

Take off your wedding ring right away. **Ouch!** You can always put it back on later. If that makes you uncomfortable, just take it off when your estranged spouse is around.

Next, make sure you keep up the house. You want to show that you can hold it all together in times of crisis. **Ouch!**

Next, look your best whenever you answer your door and always have some place to be. **Ouch!** Even if you don't, at least grab your keys and drive around the block.

The goal is to get your spouse's feelings to surface before it is too late. He or she isn't thinking about the future and all the ramifications of divorce. These little doses of reality might awaken something inside. We want them to feel the Ouch Factor.

WHEN IS IT TOO LATE?

When is it too late? I remember thinking someone has to get through to him before he sleeps with her and ends our marriage. That was my boundary. I was racing against time before he threw it all away. I pointed out that someday there would be another man in his house, raising his children, mowing his lawn, sleeping in his bed, and escorting his daughter down the aisle.

To the cheater, having sex is not necessarily the defining act that ends the marriage.

My perception was that my husband chose to end the marriage by sleeping with another woman, but I later learned his perception was very different from mine. About seven years after our divorce, another member of my family went through a similar divorce. Her husband was having an affair. She asked me if my ex would call her husband and just talk to him about the road ahead. When I asked my ex, I explained that she was in panic mode, a feeling I remember all too well, and wanted to reach her husband before he slept with this other woman and it was too late. Jim replied, "*She's* the one who decides if it's too late." Without saying so, he implied that I had filed for a divorce too soon. I never knew that he wasn't ready to end the marriage, even after having sex with someone else. In other words, to the cheater, having sex is not necessarily the defining act that ends the marriage. Cheaters have already decided it is over or they are just running amuck waiting for their feelings to come back. However, if you are the victim and the one betrayed, it's a different story.

I thought it was very telling that Jim never made the call. His second reply to me about what her husband was doing was what one would expect from an older and wiser warrior reflecting on his past battles. He said, "He'll regret it."

My old neighbor said it best: "There are no rules right now." It was true. All the boundaries I had set in my mind and all the consequences I had laid out became fuzzy during the six months that preceded the divorce. I learned that I could forgive and overlook my own boundaries, but in the end the ultimate issue was trust and the original boundaries prevailed.

When a cheating spouse takes us for granted and chooses to be with someone else, they get what they get and there are no guarantees after that. My oldest sister explained it to me like this. She and her husband had affairs. Once that happened, they could never dance in step to the music again.

DEALING WITH THE MISTRESS

Dealing with the "other" woman can be unnerving to say the least, but you can get through it, if you just use a little psychology.

43. Women who cheat with married men are weak minded and extremely insecure.

Knowing this will give you the upper hand. The way to get even with the mistress is to mess with her mind. The best way is to be very normal and level headed from a distance. In other words, smile and get along with others around you, she will be watching from afar. It will make her wonder why your husband left you. After she figures out it wasn't entirely your fault, she will become insecure and drive him away with her own jealousy and insecurity.

44. Maintain class at all times.

The best way to deal with a mistress who thinks she is a princess is to avoid any communication with her after you've gotten your confirmation. The environment is too rich with emotion and it could be unsafe. If you don't, you might say or do something you will regret and it will bring you down to her level. Just remember, once she is attached to your husband, she will stake her claim because she has to; She took something that didn't belong to her. Let her have the tiara and instill a personal "code of silence". She will figure out on her own that it's not what she thinks it's cracked up to be. You will hold the crowned jewels forever if you always maintain class.

We've all heard about the scorned ex-wife who confronts the mistress with a slap in the face. Sure, it might feel really good, but why stoop to her level. Don't give her anything, least of all your control, to make her feel better than you.

You might slip once or twice and if this happens don't beat yourself up over it. Just move on and chances are she will do ten classless acts to your one anyway.

45. When the mistress shows up with your ex to pick up the kids, remember to breathe.

You're in shock. What the heck? Why is she here? Airflow reduces stress and anxiety, so just breathe, air, not fire! When my wounds were still raw and she came with him to pick up my children, I made it very uncomfortable for her. I would walk out and greet her with a forced smile and then politely remind her that he would leave her like he found her. This was my first slip up and was contrary to showing class at all times. Later, I realized she only came because she didn't trust him to be alone with me. There was power in that once I figured it out. Eventually she stopped coming and put him on a stopwatch!

46. Once a mistress attaches herself to a married man she needs constant reassurance from him that he isn't going to go back to his wife.

I used to get phone calls at work from someone who would hang up when I said hello. This happened a lot. I thought it was her checking up on him through me. If I was absent that day, there was a possibility in her mind that I was with him. In an odd way this gave me strength. She was getting a taste of her own medicine, and I had absolutely nothing to do with it because by this time, he and I were ancient history.

47. Take care of yourself and give her a reason to be jealous

When you're the one who's been cheated on, it's only natural to feel a twinge of jealousy. Not only did I feel a twinge, I couldn't even look at women who resembled her. But what you do with yourself after your ex splits is essential. Before he left, I have to admit, I was feeling and looking a little frumpy. After he left I grew my hair and lost some weight. I felt better about myself, and it helped me to mentally even up the score.

48. The best revenge is to live well.

Looks aren't everything. It's also important to live well and take care of yourself. By that I mean live within your means, take care of your possessions (house and car), and surround yourself with good supportive people.

Pamper yourself. Now is the time to take care of you. How else can you take care of others. Drink lots of water. You will need it from all the tears you have cried. Take a good multi-vitamin. Get your rest and plenty of exercise. Even if you just get out of the house after dinner for a short walk, it will change your frame of mind. Get a massage when you can afford one. Having the tactile touch of another in a soothing way can do wonders for the body and soul. If shopping is your thing and you are on a budget, try thrift stores.

FROM THE TUELBOX

As I wind this chapter down, I just want to leave you with this. If your spouse ever leaves you for someone else, they will eventually be sorry, sincerely. You will get an apology, one way or another. It may or may not be verbally spoken, but you will know it and see it and so will others.

The School of Hard Knocks has a term for your ex's condition when this happens; it's called Cognitive Dissonance (i.e. Buyer's Remorse). You will learn about it in your next required course on Consumer Behavior. For our non-majors (or those of you who cheated) there is a class for you, too. The degree program center will allow you to substitute your Consumer Behavior class for an Agriculture class. It's called, **Grass No Greener***.

  *Prerequisites:
  - **Growing a Beanstock Marriage – Jack's Way**
  - **Getting In Touch With Your Green Thumb.**
  - **Landscape Restoration**

6

Fight Or Flight

YOU'VE PROBABLY HEARD OF the fight or flight theory. I think I first learned about it in high school biology. The theory, originally discovered by Harvard physiologist Walter Cannon, goes like this:

> The Fight or Flight response is an instinctive, genetic reaction we have to bodily harm. When under stress or endangered, our bodies prepare us for the fight or flight response mode. We undergo a series of very dramatic changes when threatened. We begin to breathe faster, the blood from our digestive system is diverted to our muscles and limbs for running and fighting, our pupils dilate, our awareness intensifies, our sight sharpens, our impulses quicken, and our perception of pain diminishes. We become ready to fight or flight. *(Neil Neimark, M.D., online http://www.thebodysoulconnection.com/Education-Center/fight.html)*

According to the theory, we developed this response back in the days of saber tooth tigers. It was our body's way of telling us to run like the wind when danger was near, but what Dr. Cannon didn't tell us was that this reaction to bodily harm actually started in the cave.

Imagine for a moment what it would have been like back then. Let's travel together back in time 4 million years ago. It's a beautiful Saturday. You're a little punchy from the clubbing you took from Caveman Al last night, but all is forgiven as it was Al's little way of saying "I love you." A little rap on the head with his club is something all the girls wanted. You're still feeling the burning love and the afterglow as you make your way back, a bit dazed still, to your favorite shady palm. When suddenly, out of nowhere, a giant caveman-eating lizard appears. In an instant you bolt back to Al's for refuge, but when you arrive Al isn't there. He's across the way, at Cavewoman Claire's. Al wants to tell Cavewoman Claire how he loves her, too. At this point, you begin to feel something impulsive come over you and within a split second you are ready to kick some caveman ass. Poor Al didn't see it coming.

Maybe this isn't exactly the kind of threat that Dr. Cannon meant, but nonetheless I bet caveman Al knew danger was near and eminent. The Fight or Flight response is primal, and it has evolved. Let me show you what I mean.

THE DECISION TO FIGHT AND THE WAYS WE DO IT

Take the case of a woman married to a consultant that came to work with me. He was well liked and very professional. I had found him very easy to work with. He was married and had children and I knew his wife did not work for our organization. Several months into his contract, I noticed him having lunch and spending time in the parking lot after work with another female employee. The body language alone said it all: they were having an affair. A few years later, I found out my observations were correct. What was amazing to me was that he was still with his wife. A friend told me that after his wife found out about the affair, she decided to go to war. She was determined to fight for her

husband with all of her womanly powers. She and my girlfriend had become good friends and I will never forget how
my girlfriend explained this woman's story.

In order to keep her husband, this woman decided she
needed to start taking an interest in the things that interested
him. She started taking up fishing, skiing, and cycling so that
she could have more in common with him. She was determined not to let this other woman take away what she and
her husband had built their lives around. She was going to
win him back with love and kindness. Her plan worked, and
he ended the affair. They had to work on healing together,
but they had a rejuvenated relationship.

Most women would not put themselves through what
this exceptional woman did to save her marriage. Most self-
respecting women would just hand him divorce papers. But
who is to say what is right or wrong in relationships. The
unanswered question is: how did she know it was right for
her to stay and fight? That's something we must answer for
ourselves. My only word of caution to someone in her shoes
is: make sure you are fighting to save your relationship for
the right reasons and not just to win. The right reason to
fight is because you love your spouse and want to rebuild the
love you once shared.

I will say it again: don't fight just to win. You will be disappointed in the end. There is no doubt that egos are badly
bruised when someone's actions say, "I don't choose you any
more; Instead I choose her or him." The natural reaction is
to compete on any level just to win. But by competing you
set up an adversarial relationship. Competition is good for
some things, like sports, but not for relationships. When you
compete in a relationship for someone's love, you lose sight
of the goal. If you fight with love, the goal remains in view.

49. The only way to fight <u>for</u> love is to fight <u>with</u> love.

The exceptional woman in the story fought her battle
with love and determination. She wasn't vindictive towards
the other woman; she was above her. Using love to fight your
battles puts you in a position of power. Maintaining class
and dignity will put you in a higher league than the other
woman. She can't sling mud if there is no dirt. Instead, in
time, she will internalize all she did to you and wonder why
you have his heart and she doesn't.

Don't confuse 'fighting love with love' with being passive
and being taken advantage of either. If you have been
tolerant and tried to fight to save your marriage, but your
crap meter registers "tilt," on a regular basis it's time to
regroup and try another strategy.

50. People try to fight for love the wrong way. They try to fight for love with logic.

The problem with fighting for love with logic is this:
emotions are not logical. You cannot persuade someone to
stay and love you. You cannot convince someone with words
to change how they feel.

It's the same as trying to convince a sore to heal with
words. You cannot heal a heart by convincing it to heal. You
have to treat a wound with something it will respond to. We
use antibiotics to heal our wounds. Love is the antibiotic to
heal the heart.

People try to use guilt to persuade someone to stay.
The problem with fighting for love with guilt is this: guilt
is never enough. The trouble with guilt is that they may in
fact stay, but they will resent it. And in the end, they will
leave anyway.

There are ways we fight *for* our relationship and ways we
fight *in* our relationship. One way people fight with each

other is by withdrawing. This is the "Fine, whatever, I'm not talking to you" strategy. Some of us get the silent treatment from our partner just after a fight. Just remember, that's crap. It is a passive-aggressive way of controlling the non-fight. Withdrawing doesn't take much, but the person that withdraws expects way too much from their partner. A person who withdraws is saying, "I will only communicate with you nonverbally. I challenge you to figure out why I am mad, and you better not get it wrong because you are supposed to read my mind."

The withdrawal strategy goes like this. "I'm pissed. I don't want to talk anymore. If you're lucky I might talk to you next week, but you better start kissing my ass if you want me to talk. I will control the fight through my silence and hold a grudge. As for sex? Fat chance!"

The withdrawal strategy can backfire big time. If you are on the receiving end, it can be a welcome silence. You go to your own corner and peace is had, or at least as long as you are not in the same room together. But the receiver almost always has the upper hand. The receiver can be happy because he or she is not the grudge holder. The receiver can choose to flit and float around the room ignoring the withdrawer's condition. An occasional question will be posed to make conversation, and when the withdrawer says nothing, the receiver can minimize the situation by saying, "Oh, are you still mad about that?" And by virtue of arrogance will win the fight.

The Avoidance Strategy is the Withdrawal Strategy raised to the power of ten. The Avoidance Strategy comes into play after you've been together for a long time and you adopt an attitude about the marriage of Qué Será, Será (whatever will be will be). Sometimes the best strategy is to do nothing. By doing nothing you don't react, you don't answer the phone, you don't communicate, you just go about your life as though the other person is no longer in it. There is power in silence. If you must communicate, do so in writing until you feel indifferent about the other person. Lead a single life and in doing so, you will move on. And if you are lucky your spouse will miss you enough to come after you.

My ex in-laws were pretty good at this and it worked for them. My mother-in law would get fed up with her husband and would temporarily exit the marriage. She would start a new life without her husband. No one ever worried about it though. The kids would just know, mom is going through one of her phases again. One time she moved up to the Redwoods and pursued her life long dream of running a restaurant. She settled in for a while and established residence. Before long her husband was donning an apron and cooking next to her as the fry chef. Eventually, they rekindled their marriage. It worked for them.

When you are committed to your marriage, you know your place in that marriage and you won't be mamzied-pamzied out of it. At least not without a fight. I think a lot of men, like my ex- father-in-law, find themselves clueless. He didn't know why his wife was mad at him, he just knew she was serious and he better go get her.

A friend and co-worker, Steve, was having troubles in his marriage of eight years. He and his wife married in their forties and neither had children. At their age, they knew what they were looking for in a mate. All their friends said they were perfect for each other. But when his wife had a brush with death and was recovering from cancer her outlook on life changed. Instead of being more appreciative of the gift of life and their marriage, she seemed to withdraw and become resentful toward him. He explained it to me like this, " It's as if I've done something wrong, but I can't figure out what I did to make her resent me so."

I explained to him that maybe it wasn't what he *was* doing, rather it was what he *wasn't* doing. He said he always invited her on his motorcycle outings, but she was afraid of riding and wouldn't go. I asked if he went anyway, and he said yes. I offered that he plan something she liked to do and make her do it with him. Don't accept a "no" answer and don't give up.

When people are in the Steve mode and the relationship has gotten so far off course, it is time to call in the professionals. The simple act of saying I care enough about our marriage to call a counselor, may be enough to rechart your marriage coordinates. Then again, it may not.

So when should you stay and fight for a relationship? Only you can answer that. But a good place to start is your subconscious crap meter. Have you checked it lately? Make a checklist of the crap you've put up with and the ways you can fight for the relationship. Here is how I helped Steve with his lists.

Steve's Subconscious Crap Meter

1   My wife is bitter
2   I seem to irritate her all the time
3   She won't let me close to her
4   She says I need counseling
5   My wife wants nothing to do with me
6   Nothing I do is right
7   I can't right the situation
8   She doesn't want sex

Recharting Steve's Marriage Coordinates

1   Do sweet things for her
2   Make her laugh; then make her proud
3   So back off
4   Go to counseling
5   She wants everything to do with you
6   Start by taking her hand
7   Use your imagination
8   She will eventually

Looking for the tiniest of triggers to spark movement in the direction of commitment is the goal right now. How do you do that? It's not easy and unfortunately, sometimes it just has to get worse before it gets better.

THE DECISION TO TAKE FLIGHT (WHEN IT'S TIME TO CALL IT QUITS)

A relationship is capable of digressing so much that sometimes contentment is replaced by total misery. Like the two basic fundamental emotions of a newborn infant, contentment and total misery, an unhealthy relationship knows these emotions well. Here is how these two basic fundamental emotions work in a newborn infant. There's contentment, which translates into "I'm not wet, I'm not hungry, I'm not cold, I'm just content." No more, no less. Then there's the complete opposite: "I'm miserable and I hate it so much that I'm going to scream about it as loud as I can and make sure everybody knows how much I hate it." That's it, just two extremes: content and totally miserable. I'm fine one minute, and I'm totally miserable the next.

It's funny, but a baby isn't born knowing how to laugh. Laughter is a learned behavior and takes a while to develop. First, there's a grin one day. Everybody stops in bewilderment and gathers around for the next big show, but then all excitement dissipates when you realize it is nothing more than gas. A few more weeks pass and low and behold a real smile is formed. Happiness and laughter are now new emotions for the baby.

It's kind of like this for married couples on the heels of divorce. The relationship has dwindled down to the two emotional extremes: contentment and total misery. There is no in-between. You know it's serious when you can't tell if your spouse is grinning or just has gas. That may be it on the emotional scale: contentment, misery or gas. That's all you get. When the only humor left in the relationship is gleaned from a fart, and you're the only one laughing, you know you are headed for trouble.

If a case of gas is the only thing keeping your relationship alive, it might be time to eat more beans and buy a fan. It's all about whatever works.

But, at some point in every relationship, you are bound to ask yourself, "Should I stay or should I go?" It's only natural, not disloyal, for that question to enter your thoughts. We may be completely in love with someone and still ask the question. If you imagine your life without this person and feel a pain in your heart, you know you are meant to be together. But if you ask the question and the thought of leaving brings relief, you know you have issues. Knowing when to fight for a relationship and when to give it up is not easy. There is a process to finding the answer.

Listen to your dreams. I'm a firm believer in dreams. Dreams can validate our love. I believe we have the ability to address and answer our issues in our sleep. When I was still married to my former husband and things were strained between us, I would dream about having to choose between Jim and a former boyfriend. In the beginning of my marriage, I would always choose my husband. Later, when we began to have problems, I would still choose my husband, because it was the right thing to do, but I would long for my old boyfriend. I would wake up a little shocked and baffled by my feelings.

Now that I am happily remarried, I have a variation of this dream. I dream that Todd and I are in the early stages of courting, when he tells me he wants to take a break from the relationship. In my dream, I am crushed, but when I wake up I realize that it was just a bad dream and remember how much I love him and how thankful I am that he is in my life. This dream validates my love for him.

Pay attention to what marriage is teaching you and ask, "Are we right for each other?" Marriage is one of those things that teach you about yourself. You learn more about yourself by being married to someone, than you do by being single. When you are single you don't have someone to point out all your bad habits, but when you are married and living with someone, you hear all about them.

Maybe you aren't good at knowing what you want. Marriage will teach you what you don't want. You may learn that the sound of sports on TV is not what you want to hear the moment you walk in the door after working all day. Or you may prefer any background noise to the mind numbing silence that awaits after returning from an argument. Or, you may learn that when your spouse promises to tackle a major project alone, like putting in a sprinkler system or remodeling a bathroom, that you should have a predetermined completion date of less than one year established upfront.

When you are in the process of deciding if you should stay or go everything is magnified on the crap meter. Your vision is clouded because of it and irrational behavior becomes the norm around the house. Once the fits of rage, the disappearing acts, and the other disrespecting behaviors start, you both are on your way to losing the respect of each other for good. If you've reached the point of no return and you simply don't care, then sit back because you won't enjoy the ride.

After one of you breaks the sonic barrier and takes your marriage on this path, it doesn't matter what comes next. Your marriage will gravitate in the direction it is most committed to. If you are both committed to ending it, then that is the direction it will head. If you are both committed to saving it then you will fight accordingly. If you are not on the same page, then time will decide your fate.

51. Fighting for the relationship alone is like trying to move a rainbow

Sometimes, we are so hell-bent on saving the relationship we lose ourselves in hopeless optimism. We convince ourselves we can move rainbows. This was my story (as told in Chapter 2). So we try and try and get nowhere. Or sometimes it is simply fear that keeps us working at the relationship and hoping it will get better. We are afraid to quit or give up. We feel we have to continue the fight, for our children, for our families, for our church, etc. I'm here to tell you it is okay to let go of the toxic relationship in your life. If the relationship is meant to be, it will be some other time. You can't force it.

52. It's time to check out when your spouse has stopped checking in.

During your decision making process you may decide that the relationship isn't worth fighting for any more. If you find yourself fighting a losing battle, it is time to question "why" and consider surrender. Why are you fighting for the relationship? Why are you so convinced this person is the only other person in the world for you? Why would moving on be so devastating? Why are you afraid of letting go? Why don't you feel you deserve to be loved? Why are you holding on?

STATISTICS ON MARRIAGE LONGEVITY

Before you throw in the towel let me just enlighten you. Anyone who has been married for more than 5 minutes understands what it is like to go through phases of not liking your own spouse. Now the longer you are married the longer these phases might be. Don't feel privileged if you think not liking your spouse for 3 weeks is a long time. I know people who say they didn't liked their spouse for years and then one day their relationship turned around.

The statistics on longevity of marriages is something to note. According to the U.S. Census Bureau, the percentage of married people who reach their 5th, 10th, and 15th anniversaries are as follows:

5th   : 82%
10th : 65%
15th : 52%

The percentages show that almost half of all marriages call it quits by the 15th year.

Lets look at the percentages for those marriages reaching their 25th, 35th, and 50th anniversaries:

25th : 33%
35th : 20%
50th : 5%

Only 5% of marriages see their 50th wedding anniversary. So the next time you attend someone's golden anniversary you will know how rare an event it truly is.

A colleague of mine explained to me that he and his wife could have easily been divorced four or five times over the course of their twenty-five years together, but they could have also been remarried that many times, too. Having a marriage last the test of time, he told me, is hard work emotionally, takes faith — and an extra bedroom never hurt.

53. Conflicts can be used as a way to get closer.

According to the Coalition for Marriage Family and Couples Education the number one predictor of divorce is the habitual avoidance of conflict. Couples who are of the mindset that arguments will ruin their marriage have it all wrong. Because they haven't learned how to fight effec-

tively, they fear a fight will be too destructive to the marriage.
Fighting becomes too risky to them. So they hold it in until
eventually they start to shut down.

The Coalition for Marriage Family and Couples Education
found the following to be true of successful marriages:

1.   Successful couples have the same number of disagree-
     ments as couples who divorce.
2.   Every happy successful couple have approximately
     ten areas of "incompatibility" or disagreement that
     they will never resolve.
3.   Success of a marriage rests in the way the couples
     handled their conflicts.

Couples whose marriages endure have learned to use
conflict in their marriages as a way of getting closer. Still,
many couples don't realize that having conflict is healthy.
When you resolve the conflict and make up it is important
to understand each other's upsets and fears. It's not enough
just to make up. That's what we all like to do. You've got to
use this time to get to the core of the issue and in this way
you will learn more about each other. It will make future
conflicts less traumatic and you will be freer in your marriage
to have disagreements.

When you lack the communication skills necessary to
convey your feelings, you lose your voice in the marriage.
What happens is you seek validation from someone outside
the marriage. When you do this, you are really cheating
yourself because you are hiding from the issues with your
partner. Sure, it is easy to get confirmation from unrelated
parties that you are not the one with the problem, but you
need to use conflict as a means to an end. Resolving conflicts
with your partner will bond you tighter as a couple. This was
something I had to learn.

People don't see conflict as an opportunity to get closer, and consequently, they don't use it to their advantage. Instead people avoid conflict and hedge the confrontation. When you force yourself to discuss why you have opposing views and see things from your spouse's perspective, you gain insight to his or her logic and fears. Through understanding, you can alleviate your partner's fears and reach a mutual agreement. It draws you closer together when you know, I mean really know, that you can work things out. I am over simplifying this a bit, but the bottom line is we need to learn to communicate without fear. It takes awhile to learn this, and some people never do. It wasn't until my second marriage that I figured this out.

Conflict resolution is a learned skill and can require the guidance of a trained professional. It is money well spent.

YOU DROPPED A BOMB ON ME, BABY

For everyone who has ever been through a divorce you have either had a bomb dropped on you or you did the bombing. Being on the receiving end of the announcement and hearing that your spouse wants out is devastating. If you are the one announcing that the marriage should end there is never a right moment.

My girlfriend explained how the bomb was dropped on her. It was their 13th wedding anniversary. Her husband came home with flowers and out of nowhere dropped the news that he didn't love her anymore and wanted to leave. She hadn't a clue he was unhappy, and there was no convincing him to go to counseling. Their anniversary was in January and by mid March he still hadn't left. Meanwhile, she was on anti-depressants and was trying to hold it together so the kids wouldn't find out.

Unfortunately, this is an all too common episode in American families. The bomb gets dropped and there is no realistic plan of action. Her husband thought he had it all figured out, but after sitting down and looking at the finances he realized he couldn't afford to move out, so he stayed.

According to my girlfriend, things seemed to improve. She gave him space and he seemed to be free with the hello kiss and some affections. It led her to think he was having a change of heart. For Valentines Day he even brought her a dozen red roses and a card that said, "Love, Peter." But three weeks later, when she asked if he was reconsidering he flatly said, "No, I still feel the same."

She was broken hearted. His actions gave her mixed messages and now she questioned how long he had been playing this game of charades. After his proclamation, she felt he was taking advantage of her. It took her two months, but she was finally starting to get mad and was ready to set some boundaries.

The first weeks and months following the aftermath of the bomb are by far the hardest. She explained to me that she just wanted to be home with her family to hang on to their last days together. It is overwhelmingly hard, but you have to snap out of it. During this time your focus has to be on you. Setting your boundaries and standing up for yourself in the marriage is the best thing you can do.

DEFINING YOUR "END-ITS"

Everyone has their "end-its" or boundaries that will end their marriage in divorce. Usually we never have to verbalize or define what our boundaries are until someone encroaches upon them. Most people just keep a mental note of what will end a relationship for them and if your partner reads your crap meter right, they will never have to ask. It's important to air your boundaries early and eliminate any confusion. Not just for them, but for you.

For some, an "end-it" might be:

- If you get arrested one more time, we're through!
- If you come home one more time smelling like a brewery, we are done!
- If you ignore me one more time, I'm out of here!
- If your story doesn't check out, that's it!
- If you want out, just say the word, then leave!

Letting your partner know your "end-its" is important. He or she can't work in a vacuum. I don't remember how we got on the subject, but I do remember early on in our marriage defining what would end the marriage for me. We were having a calm and casual conversation when I told Jim the two things would end the marriage for me: one, if he asked for a divorce and two, if he were to see someone else. It was powerful when I had to put those words on the table for real. I had long ago set the boundaries, and he had crossed them. I remember saying, "Do you remember long ago when I told you what would end this relationship for me?" It put everything back on him.

SEPARATION OR DIVORCE?

In California, you can legally separate before filing for an actual divorce. The reason most people file a legal separation is to end financial ties to their spouse from the date of legal separation. Breaking all financial ties is a good idea because you will not be legally responsible for any debts your spouse creates after the time you separate. It is not cheap to maintain two households. As soon as one person moves out, suddenly there is a new bed to buy, new linens, rugs, towels, etc. that only one of you will ever use.

54. Get it Over Fast

So, does filing for legal separation make sense? In my opinion, no. It's just a huge waste of time because you can accomplish the same thing by filing for divorce. Yeah, bring it on! Some people file a legal separation because they don't know if they really want to be divorced. It is a trump card, if you ask me. Go ahead and file the papers. You still have time to change your mind.

Filing for divorce shows your spouse you are serious. It puts you in the driver's seat, setting the pace of the divorce. It will speed the process along, and you will heal and recover faster. Honestly, if you are not ready to get divorced – if you need to be smacked in the face with another frying pan – then don't file anything. Filing for a legal separation because you are confused will just make matters worse. Do something decisive for once in your life and move on from the idiot who's dragging you down. I don't see much point in a legal separation. In my opinion, it keeps you stuck in emotional limbo.

Prolonging the inevitable divorce is masochistic; just get it over. Drawing it out is analogous to this little story about Weimaraner puppies. A man adored his Weimaraner so much that he decided to breed her. When the puppies came along, he sadly realized he had to cut off their tiny tails to keep them true to breed. Since he hated to cause anyone that much pain, he thought, "Maybe instead of chopping the tails all off at once, I can just cut them off an inch at a time."

Unfortunately, cutting a marriage off a little at a time is more painful than ending it all at once, but that's what many of us do. After that first year, there was nothing left that would have shocked me. I took all my hits at once; Yes, it hurt, but it was over, and I was able to move on faster. So will you.

55. Don't fight over the furniture you will just replace it anyway.

Prolonging the process of divorce is what some people do to keep connected. Some will hold on to tangible things from the marriage as a way of staying connected too, tangible things that they will eventually give to charity.

Anything that reminds you of your first marriage will probably go to Goodwill or in the trash at some point (it won't sell for much in a garage sale), so let the petty stuff go.

When it comes to bills racked up by your spouse, and who pays for what, I learned to put these two little letters together: BK. That's the finance profession's abbreviation for bankruptcy. Suddenly it is a dead issue, because your half of the foregone debt is now their sole responsibility. **Blam-blam!** If bankruptcy goes against your beliefs, don't worry, you will eventually pay the debt off, but either way keeping good credit may be a challenge.

FROM THE TUELBOX

If you decide to take flight, the process you go through to reach this decision is not easy. Just because your marriage failed doesn't make you a failure. If you lose the battle it doesn't mean that you lost everything, except perhaps a problem. In fact, you probably gained more than you lost. It takes time to realize this, but it is true. You are victorious in your efforts if you come off of the battlefield wiser, more humble, more compassionate, and more forgiving. And your next love will be more evolved because of it.

Remember this one thing, winners know when to quit.

7

Getting to Indifference

THE OPPOSITE OF LOVE isn't hate; it's indifference.
I first heard this statement when I was 20-years-old and
going through my first major heartbreak. The young man
involved, Brett, was full of anger because of the way I ended
the relationship, and I couldn't say that I blamed him. Prior
to our relationship, I was involved with someone else and I
hadn't fully achieved closure before Brett and I started to
date. After a fifteen-month relationship with Brett, I received
a letter from my ex-boyfriend, Mitch, telling me how much
he missed me. I decided before I could ever commit to Brett
I needed to explore my feelings for Mitch. I responded to
his letter and before I knew it he was at my doorstep, the
doorstep Brett and I shared. At that age I wasn't mature
enough to handle my own feelings, let alone the feelings
of someone else. Brett and I broke up after I confessed my
state of confusion.

He was terribly hurt and at first I was left regretting what
I had done to him. Later, I regretted what I had done to
myself. I learned that Mitch wasn't serious about me and
I was fool-hearted. The amazing thing is, I wouldn't have
changed anything about the experience. It taught me how
important it is to get closure. Thankfully, it was a lesson I
learned at a very young age. Some people don't learn this

lesson until later in life when there is more at stake, like a
spouse, a few kids, and a mortgage.

Brett wouldn't speak to me for two years. I thought his
anger meant he had no more feelings for me. I changed
that opinion when I fully understood that the opposite of
love isn't hate. If he hadn't loved me so much, he wouldn't
have been so angry. If he was indifferent, he wouldn't care.
In a demented way, this new insight gave me hope. I guess I
figured as long as he still felt something, there was a chance
of reuniting. I was a hopeless romantic!

Closure in a relationship comes in many forms, usually
unexpectedly. You don't even realize when it is happening;
you just know it when you have achieved it. It is like healing
from any wound. There is a pestering soreness until one day
you realize you have healed. Closure is like that, except it is
a mental wound not a physical one.

Sometime after my divorce, I met up with Brett. I still
held a spark for Brett after some 12 years. Through the years
Brett and I had talked on occasion, but I had only seen him
once during my marriage. I had met him at a restaurant six
months after I was married. He slow danced with me in the
parking lot and told me he was still in love with me. I still
had feelings for him, but I was committed to my marriage
and had learned my lesson. It was a confusing time, to say
the least, but I knew I had to be faithful to my husband and
put Brett behind me.

Every two years or so, Brett and I would talk, mostly about
our marriages and our children. Then, one day, he told me
he was divorced. He never asked me to leave my husband
and he never told me again that he still loved me. Instead,
he apologized for causing me so much confusion. Slowly,
through these conversations, I got small doses of closure.

Seven years after that dance in the parking lot, my
husband and I divorced. I thought about seeing Brett and

whether we could rekindle the relationship. For years, I had
thought that maybe we were supposed to be together.

About a year later, we spoke, but he was in a committed
relationship and seemed in love. When I finally did see him,
we had a pleasant time talking and catching up, but to my
surprise, the spark was gone. A few weeks later, I realized I
no longer had a compelling urge to call him.

56. When you have a mental image of your ideal and you finally come face to face with that ideal, you will realize that your imagination lacks what the rest of your senses are able to discern.

By coming face to face with Brett, all my senses came
together and formulated the conclusion that I finally
achieved closure.

In my divorce, closure came much faster than it did
with Brett. I saw Brett only a few times after our relationship ended. Because Jim and I had children together, I was
forced to face my fears and deal with him often. Just seeing
him disturbed me, but it got easier in time. If I had not been
forced to see him, I might not have gotten the closure I
needed. This time, I healed in about a year- and-a-half.

57. The closer the intervals of time between doses of closure, the faster you will heal.

How long should it take to achieve closure? Closure is
very subjective, and there is no timeline. It took almost 12
years with Brett, even though our relationship only lasted
15 months, but I was over my nine-year relationship to Jim
in a year-and-a-half.

What does it feel like to have closure? Obtaining closure
is a freeing experience. You will know what it feels like when
you are no longer consumed with getting it. You will feel free,
even liberated, because it no longer holds you hostage.

DABDA

Divorce can be either of two extremes: quick and simple, or long and complicated. Whichever kind or whatever the reason, we all share the same set of emotions in getting through divorce and moving on with our lives. Even if a second party isn't involved, the sense of loss and betrayal is the same: a loss of a life promised to us, and a sense of betrayal because that promise was broken. The healing process is what you make of it. The acronym for describing the stages of grieving is DABDA. It stands for:

D – Denial	Oh, we're not having problems; she's always on the rag.
A – Anger	You saw Sandy with <u>who</u>?
B – Bargaining	If it's space you need, just let me know. Let's try to work this out.
D – Depression	My life is over. She doesn't love me any more.
A – Acceptance	I guess this is it.

It doesn't matter who left whom. We all go through these stages at different speeds and if you are like me you will bounce back and forth through them several times until you are done. If you stuff them and don't deal with them, they will eventually hit you one day and you will crash until you do. You just can't get to indifference without going through the grieving process.

I remember feeling like my ex was happy, while I was nothing but sad and depressed. I couldn't imagine him ever feeling what I was feeling. But, my girlfriend said it best. She said, you will heal 50% faster than he will because you are having these feelings now. His feelings will come. And they eventually did.

STEP INTO THE PRESENT

How can some people live in the past their whole lives, while others are able to trudge on to their next relationships without ever looking back? Those living in the past truly envy those who can put things behind them. The past-dwellers continually beat themselves up, asking, "If I had only done this or that differently, would he (or she) still be in my life?" They wonder where they went wrong. Meanwhile, the don't-look-backers freely release themselves and move forward. The difference is simply a matter of focus — a matter of timing and perspective.

58. When you are not ready to release yourself from feeling sad or guilty you will punish yourself by living in the past.

It is our conscience's way of punishing ourselves. Those that are able to move on have freed themselves from guilt and accepted that it wasn't meant to be. Believing that there will be someone else is a means to letting go of the past. Many people get stuck in the mental trap of self-pity and don't believe there will ever be another person for them. Anger, fear, stubbornness, and mistrust hold them back, as well as, a lack of self love.

Truth is, we have all been there. Everyone feels devastated at the end of a significant relationship. There is no denying the loss felt. It is a matter of putting things into perspective. I remember driving back from my hometown with my mother shortly after ending this relationship and feeling the despair of being alone. My mother poignantly pointed out to me that there are 6.5 billion people on this planet, and there is more than just one right person for each of us. She said that if people can live in the same community all our lives and find their soul mate within a 50-mile radius, the odds of finding everlasting love anywhere on the planet is highly probable. This was the first time statistics made sense to me. Nonetheless, I got the message loud and clear.

Women think men move out of the past faster than they do. But it really has more to do with practice than gender. The more you are willing to put yourself out there and experience new beginnings, the more endings you might endure, but with anything the more you do it the easier it becomes.

59. You will eventually be able to go out to the garage without thinking of him.

For a long time, I had a hard time going out to the garage without crying. It was his part of the house where things he had worked hard for were kept. When I had to go out there for something, I'd just weep. This, too, passed. It took time and will.

It is a learned behavior to move from the past to the present. This may seem obvious to many people, and yet so many of us don't know how. More likely, many people understand the concept, but refuse to try. American music icon, Ray Charles' classic hit, "I Can't Stop Loving You," says it all. Lyrics in the second verse are poignant for past-dwellers: "I've made up my mind to live in memory of the lonesome times." We have a choice – chose the present over the past.

We are all capable of moving out of the past, but some stay there longer because it is their way of remaining connected to their former partner. They disguise their longing for the past by telling themselves they can't trust anyone ever again. It sounds better than admitting that they're scared to let go of the past or have issues with fear of abandonment.

Some of the most successful business people I know recoil in fear when it comes to their personal lives. They are afraid that ending a relationship will be devastating and they can't fathom ever starting another one. So they settle. Yet, in business, fear is their motivator. They can make financial decisions with lightning speed, but they won't budge an inch to improve their love lives. They put their personal problems on the back burner and never confront them. They stay busy at work in order to ignore the problem.

It is pretty easy to figure out why. They only do what they are good at and can control. They can't accept failure, but they fail to realize that they are only failing themselves.

So how do we make this transition from past to present? How do we free ourselves from loving someone from the past? You must seek closure until you have it.

For years I have had the same discussion with a friend of mine about the men in her life. She explained that money was her security blanket. She thought money was the answer, not love, but I think her priorities were a little mixed up. I had met her husband and they didn't seem at all a likely pair. She admitted to me that she married someone that could never hurt her because she didn't marry for love. She hadn't allowed her marriage to give her security. She has let fear rob her of a better love.

I was perplexed why she could not overcome her fears. I have had the good fortune to meet Dr. Stephen Covey, an international authority on leadership and values, who explained it to me like this: People consumed by fear need to have a person with whom they can safely confide. They just need to be heard. If someone they trust listens, they will eventually get tired of their own issues, but they have to come to this conclusion themselves. In so doing they will find their own closure.

SEEKING "PRIVATE" CLOSURE

60. You will learn how important closure is.

You need to seek closure with militant perseverance. It is scary to face our fears. No one knows fear better than the commando ex who meets an old lover one last time for confirmation and closure. No matter how fearful it may be, now is the time to earn your metal of valor for bravery. Life is too short to live in the past.

61. Closure can come quickly or slowly, but I believe closure comes in doses. You have to seek out your own comfort level.

I remember how brave Kathy, my friend's roommate, was when she went to see her ex-boyfriend after a year-long cooling-off period. After a seven-year relationship, he had dumped her for another woman and was very cold about it. Since their breakup, she had graduated from law school, passed the bar exam and was doing well. By all outward appearances she had moved on and wanted him to know it. In reality, she desperately needed closure, or at least a dose of closure.

Her goal was to make him regret what he had done, and she didn't hold back. With all her womanly ammunition and dressed for war, she looked like a new recruit for the Girl With a Mission Army. Standard-issue apparel consisted of a pink Dior Couture-tailored suit and Cole Haan stiletto heels for combat boots. She looked stunning and was ready for battle. They met for coffee at 0900 hours. She could have knocked him dead, but unfortunately she didn't get closure. She was still hurting deep inside, and the meeting was outside her comfort zone. She got a dose of closure, but she still needed more. Through the years, she found ways to get more closure, but she never confronted her heart's capturer again.

Occasionally she would hear about him through friends until one day she read an article about him in the paper. It was an article praising his success as a community small business owner. Included in the article was a picture of him with his family. She saw the wife he had chosen, the kids he had raised and the community where he lived. Though she was glad for him, she realized how different their lives were and she was finally able to put that piece of the past behind her.

62. One of the best gifts a current lover can give is to allow the troubled partner the freedom to get closure from a past relationship.

Sometime after my divorce, Jack, an ex-boyfriend from college who worked in television invited me to the station to watch a taping. I thought our meeting was innocent and nothing more than two old friends catching up. I exchanged emails with Jack, and 10 months later, I received a call from Jack's wife, accusing me of having an affair with her husband. I tried to relieve her of any suspicion, but it was no use. She was convinced that there was something more to it. Then, it started to add up. Jack had said he never expected to see me again and that he never really had a chance to say good-bye.

He had never fully gotten the closure he needed before he married, and it was affecting his relationship with his wife. If he could have been open and honest with his wife (before he married her), he might have been able to see me again and freely get the closure he needed. But, instead I remained the forbidden fruit and a temptation to him in some way. I am not advocating that if your partner still has feelings for someone, you should let them pursue it. My point is that you need to resolve your past relationships before having a serious and committed relationship with someone else.

When I was dating my husband, Todd, we would get close to a commitment, but then he would back out of it. This went on for sometime. We finally realized that unresolved feelings for an ex-girlfriend were holding him back. It was hard to do, but I told him he needed to go see her and find out what his true feelings were. This was one of the best things I ever did for us. I backed out of his life for a time, and later when we reconnected he told me he had gone to see her and the feelings weren't what he expected. This seemed to free him. It also freed me of wondering if she was still in control of his heart. As a result, we were able to move forward in our relationship.

Fears of not having closure can surface when we get serious with someone new, especially as we get older and take our commitments more seriously. Falling in love tends to scare us on many levels and can awaken our doubts about deserving happiness. We question how anyone can love us as much as we love them. Does this person even exist and if so do I deserve them. We question our own ability to make them happy and do good in the relationship. It's a huge self confidence thing.

IS GETTING CLOSURE LESS COMMON THAN YOU THINK?

Wondering about someone is normal and does not necessarily mean you lack closure. I'm always surprised by the innocence of people who married young and have remained together. It is refreshing to say the least. Charlie had been married for thirty years and had married young. Although he had asked a general question about closure with ex girl-friends, I could tell he secretly wondered about someone from the past. He simply wondered who this person was, who they became, and what did they look like now. Pretty harmless stuff. I tried to reassure him that was pretty normal human curiosity and it didn't mean he didn't have closure.

Not having closure only gets in the way of a new relationship when it distracts us mentally and draws us to act on old feelings. That's not good. Take the case of Jay and the hook up call.

THE HOOK UP CALL

63. You will experience the difference between the hook up call and the bootie call.

Everyone has experienced "the call" at some point in life. I'm not talking about the "bootie call," which usually comes late at night with only one purpose, to get some "bootie." The "hook up" call comes unexpectedly during the waking hours from an "ex," looking for a status check of your love life. The sole motive is to find out if you are seeing anybody, and if not, if you can hook up again.

Like anything, the more you understand about the nature of such calls, the better. My experience has been that if the relationship ended because your partner was not ready for a commitment, and you treated him or her with respect, chances are you will be the receiver of a "hook up call".

The "hook up call" usually comes within six months to two years after the end of a relationship. The closer the call comes to the six month mark, the more sincere the caller is about rekindling the relationship. The closer to the two-year mark the less sincere, and after two years, it's probably just a bootie call.

In most cases, the caller's intentions to get back together are sincere. You must step back and evaluate what is happening. But that is not so easy right then and there.

You are overwhelmed with excitement, anger, confusion, and curiosity. It's hard to imagine that the ringing of the telephone can awaken so many feelings.

When Jay decided to get over Terry, he took up Internet dating with a vengeance. After several tries, he met Nan and their relationship took off. After several months of "moving on" from Terry and "moving forward" with Nan, Jay got "the call."

Jay had been seeing Nan for several months, and her thoughtfulness had convinced him that the breakup with Terry was for the best. Instead of moving on by himself until he got closure from Terry, Jay chose to latch onto Nan. In doing so, he wasn't completely ready for what was about to happen.

The call came during the holidays. It was Terry. Jay contained himself and waited a few days to return the call. During this period, he was tormented with what to do. Had Jay read this book it would have saved him a lot of agony.

By the time Jay returned the call, he had enough time to reflect. He was careful not to reveal too much about his present relationship. He did this to protect Terry and also to keep the door open with her. He still wasn't completely sure that Terry wasn't for him.

By allowing himself the time to reflect on the bad experiences he had with Terry, he was able to snap out of the spell her call had placed him under. He remembered how she had hurt him so many times, how she treated him when he confronted her about her affair, how she lied to him, how she was impatient with his pain and feelings, and all the little things she never did for him. But Jay was a guy, and he kept getting tripped up on how good the sex had been.

FALLING PREY TO THE "EX"

Without complete closure, our hearts remain prey to the ex and can be vulnerable to their whims. It's like setting yourself up to be the butt of a bad joke. Falling prey to the "ex" can leave us feeling like we want to shout a big Homer Simpson "Doh!"

Jay began to feel himself having doubts about his current relationship. Now that Terry was an option again, he was finding himself exploring his feelings for her. This was a surprise to Jay. He thought all his feelings for her were gone.

After the call he found himself more perplexed than ever about his relationship with Nan. Would he tell her about the call? Would he "hook up" with Terry over the holidays? Would he secretly seek the closure he needed or would he tell Nan this was something he needed to do so he could freely move forward in their relationship. Would she understand?

The pickle Jay got himself into is all too common. He was falling prey to the ex. What is crucial at this point is honesty. Jay and Terry had only broken up a few short months before Jay met Nan. Then after just five months, Jay was already in a semi-serious relationship with Nan. Should Nan have seen this coming? Was she naïve to assume Jay was over this other woman?

WHAT WOULD YOU DO IF YOUR EX CAME BACK TOMORROW?

Nan should have kept Jay at a distance. And Jay should have kept Nan at a distance too until both partners had "the talk" together. The talk is usually started by a very poignant question that is a potential deal breaker at the beginning of any relationship: "What would you do if your ex came back tomorrow?"

There is only one right answer to this question. Your potential partner wants to hear you say you have experienced this scenario already. The potential partner will want to hear that the meeting took place, it didn't work out, and as a result you both moved on. If the scenario hasn't happened yet, then it lets your partner know that there is a very high probability that it may in the future and to proceed with caution.

Jay did what he thought was best. He met Terry for coffee. He decided to keep this from Nan until he knew how he felt. He didn't want to worry or hurt her. During coffee Terry told Jay how she had been wrong to hurt him. Finally, Jay was able to hear from Terry what he wanted to hear so many months before. After their meeting, he was more confused than ever. Should he stop seeing Nan and go back to Terry? This would break Nan's heart. Jay decided he should stop seeing Nan and give himself a break from anything serious until he could figure things out.

Except, Jay fell prey to his ex. He was vulnerable to Terry and slept with her that night, only to realize it wasn't what it used to be. Although he never mentioned this to Nan, their relationship suffered from it and gradually came to an end, too. It led Jay to question his true intentions with Nan, until finally he came to the conclusion that he rushed into their relationship.

HOW TO HANDLE THE HOOK UP CALL

Never return the hook up call immediately, even if you are so certain that this is the perfect person for you. Returning the call immediately leaves you vulnerable. You need time to reflect and gather your thoughts. There was a reason why you and this person stopped communicating, and by returning the call immediately you cast all that aside. By allowing yourself time to reflect on your past relationship, you will be more in control of your emotions. You can monitor your responses with more caution. The appropriate time to return the call is one to four days later. If you are certain you want nothing more to do with this person, wait even longer or don't return the call at all. If you are still undecided, one to four days is ample time to return the call without being rude.

Waiting says to the caller, "Hey, I'm not gaga over you anymore. I have moved on with my life without you." It will accomplish three things. One, it will make the caller feel less important in your life. Two, it will make them wonder if you have found someone else. And three, it gives you the control. Giving up this control too early can be detrimental to rekindling the spark. By waiting, you create anticipation. The longer you wait the more time they have to reflect on the relationship and why you might not be calling. It gives them time to fester in self-doubt, so that when you do finally return the call, they are not only happy to hear from you, but your call validates them. Your call says to them, okay I'm receptive to communication and I'm interested in what you have to say.

DON'T SPILL THE BEANS

When you do call, just remember, you can't say the wrong thing to the right person, but let them go first. They initiated the communication; let them say why they called and practice listening. You will have your turn.

Usually, we do one of three things. One, we either reveal with too much honesty how we have not completely moved on; two, we try and protect our past lover from the truth that we are involved with someone else (thus keeping the door open); or three, we candidly share how our new love is perfect for us.

SO HOW DO YOU GET CLOSURE WITHOUT LEAVING THE ONE YOU LOVE?

Having thoughts of someone from the past doesn't mean you are still in love with them. Sometimes, closure has to come in doses before you can get completely unstuck. Some people think the guiltier they feel about having these thoughts, the more they are still hung up on that person. Guilt can't really be used as universal measure. Some people may feel extremely guilty for just thinking about calling an old flame, while someone else would do it without batting an eye.

How you pick your method of closure can be important to the success of your current relationship. If you have started a new relationship, but have still not decided what or who you want, it is best you go your separate ways for awhile and see what the future holds. That way nobody gets hurt. Sometimes we just need to come face to face with someone from the past to get the resolution we need. It truly can be that simple.

FROM THE TUELBOX

If you are ever to achieve indifference toward your ex, you have to face your fears, which means you are going to have to deal with your ex. Closure will come in doses, and it will be uncomfortable at first. If you have children together, closure may come faster because you will be forced to deal with one another. Just remember, not getting closure before establishing your next serious relationship will eventually suck you under. The School of Hard Knocks knows this is when you will be ready for your first sink-or-swim test. The lesson to study is entitled, "How to Survive a Rip Tide."

8

Being Rejuvenated – Beyond Your Comfort Zone There Is No Mattress

D IVORCE IS A PROCESS, and you just have to let it takes its course. In other words, it ain't over 'til it's over. It is a sucky time and extremely stressful. All of us who have been divorced know this, and we cut all newcomers to the club some slack. But, we also know that things will change for the better, and that too is a process; It's called being rejuvenated! Here's how it works.

64. There is never a mattress at the end of your comfort zone.

Growth and change are never comfortable; so don't expect to find a mattress at the end of your comfort zone. My rule of thumb is: The more uncomfortable you are, the more you are going to grow. When you stretch yourself outside your comfort zone, you grow because it connects you to new experiences. With each success, you achieve a new sense of transformation.

For me stepping outside my comfort zone meant getting in front of people. One of my big fears used to be public speaking, but I made myself do it. After every successful speaking engagement, I got a little more comfortable doing it, and it became easier for the next time.

Our souls can also be rejuvenated after having a first time or a once-in-a-lifetime experience. My most recent such experience was my 20-year high school reunion. Your 20ᵗʰ high school reunion only comes around once in a lifetime. I was extremely nervous about seeing all my old friends. Would they remember me? Would I make a good impression? I was fearful, but wanted to make it a success. The experience was something I will remember for the rest of my life. Reunions are good soul food anyway. I remember being afraid of showing up alone. I knew it would ease my nerves if I reconnected with some old friends first. I arrived with a very old and dear friend. Together, we faced our evening with anticipation and excitement. After the reunion, we talked and laughed about the night's events and awkward moments shared.

At various points throughout the reunion we shuffled by each other with the intention to stop and catch our breath. But the way reunions work is you take 2 steps and there's another person you haven't seen in twenty years. You stop, say something stupid from the past to get them to remember you and turn and go on to the next person. After a few successes with good natured banter, you inevitably will come to that one person you just can't place or you can place them and neither one of you can think of anything to say, so you just shuffle on. When this happened to me it was with one of the most popular girls from our class. There was an awkward lull, so I stopped and exchanged a hello, and just like I was back in 10ᵗʰ grade she didn't try to engage me in conversation. I assumed she couldn't place me. I became disinterested in trying to work so hard at the conversation and moved on. It was in that moment that I felt freed from any high school status. It didn't matter that someone with a high status in school accepted me or not. I was comfortable with who I was.

The high school status thing changes as you mature, and everyone becomes equal. For some people who have held on to old limiting beliefs about themselves, beliefs that were established back in high school, experiencing a high school reunion can mend the soul.

The other amazing soul catching experience from a high school reunion is that you come away with a greater appreciation of these people. These are the people in life, your peers, that grow old with you.

65. Your physical appearance will change.

Stress changes us physically. I remember looking in the mirror and thinking I was aging rapidly from this ordeal. I seemed to have more gray hairs, and wrinkles appeared in places they weren't before. This change happened over a short period of time, too, maybe six months. But once you find inner peace and realize you are going to be okay, your appearance will change again. You become calm again, and people will remark how you look happier. It will show in your skin, your hair, your eyes, your smile, and even your walk.

66. Your anger will propel you to find happiness if you work with it.

In the midst of divorce you have a lot of anger. You are angry at the circumstances of your life; Angry for the disappointment of a failed marriage; Angry that your best years for sex are passing you by.

Anger can be a powerful tool when channeled in the right direction. When you turn your anger into productive energy, it can help you, not drain you. Rise to the challenge and find what works for you. Some might exercise, others might journal, fix things around the house, find a needy cause to help, do crafts, or paint, etc.

The best therapy I ever had was painting my bathroom walls. On the very weekend that my divorce was to be final, I was alone and decided to keep myself busy with a painting project. As I reveled in the moment about the significance of the date, a bittersweet feeling came over me. Bitter because our marriage had to end like this and sweet because I was finally free again. Somewhere between the bitter and the sweet I found myself angry. This is when the idea hit me. Before I knew what I was doing, my paintbrush was in hand and I was out of control. I discovered that a wall is a big canvas for profanities! All I can tell you is, when I was done I felt energized and smug. I let the paint dry for a day, a socially acceptable timeframe for the profanities to remain, and each time I walked by, I just laughed at my madness. It worked and I was happier. The bathroom came out beautiful, by the way.

67. Don't be bitter. It's unattractive and your face will freeze that way.

Being angry is normal, and you need to work through it. People expect you to be hurt and angry, but they are less tolerant of bitterness. It's something you have more control over. You can bite your tongue and monitor what comes out of your mouth. I mention this to spare you the embarrassment I endured.

I never will forget the time I was at a party seated around a table of family and friends. Someone had asked me, "How are things going?" It was a loaded question at that time in my life. So I blurted out a few things about my divorce. Just as I finished, one of the elders of the group gave me this pearl..."Don't be bitter." At the time I thought I was being funny trying to mask my anger, but instead it came across as sarcasm and bitterness. I sat up and took notice of the faces around me. All had turned away.

Just so you know, you will see beauty in life again sooner than you think and the bitterness will be sweetened with the rising of each new day. It just takes time.

68. One day you will decide you have been sad or angry long enough and you will move on. Just like that you will have a "light bulb moment."

I remember mine. I was sitting in my living room on my favorite chair where I meditated with a cup of coffee every morning. I remember thinking, "I am done crying and being angry over this. I am d-o-n-e, done." By being angry I was giving up my power to him and her. As soon as I realized that, I regained inner strength. It was as if a little light bulb in my head went on and said, "Now wait just a cotton pickin' minute." Instead of being angry at them, I got angry at myself for being angry! And because I had grown to love myself, I was able to release my anger right then and there. It was in that one moment I found the spiritual strength to move on.

Dr. Stephen R. Covey talks about this in his book, *The 8th Habit, From Effectiveness to Greatness* (Published by Free Press, copyright 2004 by FranklinCovey Co. p.44 and p.46). He says, "Anytime your emotional life is a function of someone else's weaknesses, you disempower yourself and empower those weaknesses to continue to mess your life up." In this way, "Yesterday holds tomorrow hostage." He further advocates what the American philosopher-psychologist William James taught: When we change our thinking, we change our lives.

69. Seek spirituality and your faith will grow. Even if you have never been religious before, pray. You're going to need forgiveness eventually. Amen!

It's no surprise that newly divorced couples are often full of hate and venom toward each other. It takes awhile to get past that and look inward. Through spiritual growth we come to understand our role in the divorce. It takes time, but when we open our minds to spiritual healing, clarity will come.

Divorce is a humbling experience. When we are depressed, even the simple, every day stuff can be overwhelming. All it takes is for someone to remind us that there is a God, and he never gives us more than we can handle.

As a child, religion was taught and instilled in me by my grandmother. She took it upon herself to make sure her grandchildren were at the very least exposed to church and faith. A former schoolteacher, who received her formal education at age 55, was a huge influence on my life. Though I had never considered myself a spiritual person, during my divorce I came to appreciate my grandmother's preachings of faith.

I started going to church and just listening to the message. Through the ages, human behavior hasn't changed and the stories told from the Bible gave me answers. Before I knew it I had found peace and calm. The messages and prayers gave me words to calm myself.

The Serenity Prayer was one that brought me great comfort:

God, grant me the serenity
To accept the things I cannot change,
Courage to change the things I can,
And wisdom to know the difference.

70. It is important to set time aside each day to just think.

Start by visualizing how you want your new life to be. New house, new experiences, vacations, money in the bank, a companion, etc. Dream and dream big. You are in the process of rejuvenation. Think of it as rebuilding "You Inc." Like any new company you need to have a business plan, complete with goals, objectives and budgets. Visualizing is a start, but you need to write your dreams down.

Marcia Wieder, America's Dream Coach, says this about attaining your dreams, "The quickest way to attain your dream is to have a Dream Team; people that will hold you accountable in a supportive way." Once you start speaking the goal into existence you will hold yourself accountable for the sake of your own integrity. By making strives toward fulfilling that goal you enhance your belief system about the reality of that dream. Before you know it you are on your way.

Mark Victor Hanson best selling author of *Chicken Soup for the Soul* says this about dreams:

You control your future, your destiny. What you think about comes about. By recording your dreams and goals on paper, you set in motion the process of becoming the person you most want to be. Put your future in good hands — your own.

71. You will listen to the radio again, trust me.

I had a hard time listening to the radio for awhile after my separation. Listening to the radio created anxiety that a sad song would come on and put me in a funk. It was a chance I wasn't willing to take. But eventually, I found when I was happier, that music gave me life.

72. You will go through a phase of wanting to feel sexy and attractive.

You will find that many people coming out of divorce go through a period of reclaiming who they are sexually (see Chapter 14). This is because depending on the length of your failing marriage, intimacy and feelings of being sexual were snuffed out of you.

When I was going through this phase, I decided to stop feeling so old and unattractive. I bought my first pair of thong underwear and I highlighted my hair. For someone as conservative as myself, it was enough to jumpstart the process. Next thing I knew I was wearing sports bras as outerwear. Before too long, I stopped wearing pantyhose with my sandals and as if that wasn't enough, I got really crazy and had laser surgery on my eyes. I was on a roll. I had a company motto for building "Tomi, Inc." My motto was "Get your game on!" Did I mention these little "fix me up" expenses came out of the Tomi Inc. marketing budget?

I definitely think that aspects of this phase do pass, for instance I can't stand thong underwear any more, but once your quest for feeling sexy is fulfilled you no longer have to bring yourself up from where you were sexually and you can relax. It later becomes a maintenance program of being happy with who you are again.

73. Get lots of rest. You are more emotional when you are tired.

Sleep deprivation and insomnia are directly associated with anxiety and stress. Incase you aren't sleeping very well, and chances are you aren't right now, here is my antidote. If you want to sleep soundly, – exercise. You will sleep from pure exhaustion. Then you won't be so emotional and you will look great. Working out will make you feel sexier too. Thirty minutes of moderate exercise most days is the standard recommendation for general health and a good night's rest. Studies show that exercise significantly improves sleep-quality, depression, and the quality of one's life - just look in any medical journal and you'll see.

When you exercise you will get benefits that less fit people don't enjoy. One of them is sleep. Fit people sleep more soundly than fat people. When you are fit you go into REM (Rapid Eye Movement) sleep faster and you come out of REM faster so you wake up more refreshed. Aside from the other many physiological benefits of exercise there are some other motivating reasons. Exercise results in better sex, delayed aging, increased energy and vitality, improved self-esteem, decreased body weight, and better control of hunger. Need I say more?

74. Workout—to kick some butt! Exercise is an excellent way to work off some of that hostility.

Many people complain they don't have enough time to workout, especially if they have kids. There are all kinds of gyms that cater to families. My children were 4 and 8 when I joined our family gym. They loved the gym so much that they would motivate me to go on nights I didn't feel like going. As they got older, it motivated them to do their homework. We wouldn't go unless all their homework was done first. We would get to the gym at 7:30 at night. I would work out for 45 minutes to an hour, while they played. Then in the summer, they might get to swim for 30 minutes. I would give them showers at the gym and dress them in their pajamas so that they were ready for bed when we got home. After all that activity, they were ready to sleep, and I'd still have an hour to myself after we got home. Exercise was the best medicine for all of us, hands down.

75. You will consider doing things you would have never done before.

When we are in the wrong relationship and it finally ends, our life is on a path of rejuvenation. It happens in ways we could not have imagined, but it does. The trick is to be in tune with it when it happens. For example, in my first marriage, we were homebodies. I was so dependent on my husband for my entertainment that I would never have explored trails or bike paths, much less have taken road trips on my own. When I was single I got tired of wasting time at home, so I ventured out. I took long bike rides by myself, I went jogging on the weekend to new venues, and I traveled distances just to get out and see my surroundings. One time I took a 3-hour road trip just to say I went out on Saturday night. My goal was to catch a sunset on the beach, but I got lost and missed the sunset. Nonetheless, I was out doing things and I had accomplished my mission.

When I met Todd, he and I traveled all over the state that I was born and raised in, but had never explored. There was so much to explore right in my own backyard. Things that were not part of my life before now gave my life new meaning. We went hiking on the Pacific Crest Trail on one of our adventures. We hiked with gear for two days and by the time we were finished I was exhausted, but I was also elated that I had succeeded. Todd coached and pushed me beyond my comfort zone and it was challenging.

When we are empowered in life or in a relationship, we start to change our beliefs about ourselves and our lives. The process of rejuvenation comes from redefining your zest in life.

76. In a twisted way, filing your taxes will liberate you.

I learned to embrace the fact that I was no longer filing my taxes as "Married Filing Jointly". I was now able to file as Head of Household. Just the term *Head of Household* was empowering.

Note: Simply being the head of your house does not qualify you for this filing status. Please refer to the IRS's Publication 501 for more information on this filing status.

77. You will learn to enjoy being alone.

You can learn to enjoy being alone, but it takes time to find this out. I wasn't ready for the silence in the house when the kids would go with their father on his weekends. It was all I could do not to cry. Finally, I learned to busy myself with projects, cramming as much as possible into those two days. It kept me focused and the tears away. Eventually, I used this time to recharge my mommy batteries. It was a good thing. I was able to have guilt-free time with my friends. (If you have children, this will ring a bell...Ding, dong!)

By rejuvenating your outlook on life, your situation will change. You will come out happier. If you want to jump-start the process and break out of a funk, find something that challenges you and do it. When you surround yourself with support from your "dream team" an amazing thing happens, you achieve your goals.

FROM THE TUELBOX

Being rejuvenated is not always something we consciously seek. You can find it, or it can find you. It is not the destination, but rather the journey getting there that transforms you. But if you want to find ways to change your life instead of waiting for life to change you, you have to acknowledge those things that you are afraid of or challenged by and face them. It is a three-step process. First, you need to know what your fears or challenges are; second, you need to find a way to face those fears or challenges; and third, you need to do what frightens or challenges you.

Help is there for you. All you have to do is identify your challenges and seek support. The result will be a change in what you believe about yourself, you will see.

9

When You've Gone Full Circle

THERE TRULY IS A beginning, middle, and end to a divorce.

THE BEGINNING

If you were to symbolize divorce with a circle starting at the top and arcing it down to the half waypoint, this would be the beginning to the middle. Getting around this first half is the hardest part. This is the part where the destructive secrets are revealed, the hatred breeds, and the anger sets in. You feel like the guy trying to get across the high wire on a unicycle. Back and forth you go to the circus music, inching forward, then back, then forward again, spinning your wheel. At this point, you are halfway there.

The expression, "You never really know someone until you go through a divorce," is a very true statement. Now is when you really get to know each other just a little bit better. This is the 80/20 rule in divorce. When you are married to each other, you really only reveal 80 percent of yourself. In divorce, you meet the other 20 percent. In marriage, you really only tap into your five senses. In divorce, you develop your sixth sense, the other 20 percent of who you are. You will know each other so well that you will be able to predict each other's next move. You won't have to communicate because the psychic energy between the two of you will take care of this. You will get a feeling about something, and usually you will be right. For instance if you are a guy it might happen like this: the new bubbly girlfriend giggles when she asks, "So then, she agreed to let you keep the corvette? Wow! That was really nice of her." That's when you realize you are driving the corvette, and in a flash, it occurs to you to check the brakes, only to discover as you crest the summit – there aren't any! That's what I'm talking about – developing your 6th sense.

The beginning of a divorce feels overwhelming. You go through a period of pure shock. The truth can be devastating. In my case, the truth was another woman. Like many who have been betrayed, before my marriage even ended, I was developing my sixth sense. I knew something wasn't right. You know what I am talking about if you have ever been deceived or are on the brink of divorce. It is like a psychic vibe; you just know.

Usually, you get this feeling about the time something happens. It's the time when the phone rings and you think, "Hmmm. Who would be calling him now?" Or, "Whose email address is this?"

I had a premonition about another woman two years before my husband ever cheated on me. One night, I dreamt my husband was seeing a tall skinny blonde woman and had moved into his own apartment. I woke up startled. We were on solid ground with each other, yet it seemed so real. I told my husband about it, and he reassured me that that would never happen. We both thought it was a silly dream and so I dismissed it from my thoughts. It was just so bizarre to me that I would even have this dream.

A year later my husband met her. Ten months later, something started developing between them. Suddenly, he became distant to me. I didn't understand this attitude or his shortness with me. I was beginning to see a cockiness to him.

You can imagine my shock when I learned that he was not only seeing someone, but he was seeing someone where we both worked. Amazingly, she was a tall, skinny blonde, just like the woman in my dream from two years before. True to my dream, he moved out and got his own apartment.

I was about to give the relationship what it deserved, my remaining 20 percent. Did I mention that we all have alter egos? We usually meet them for the first time when we go through a divorce. One of mine is Devilbreath Woman. She is the creature that comes out of me when I am about to breath fire and instead of fire spewing out another head pops out of my mouth, the head of Devilbreath Woman. She does this ugly gyration with her head and snaps her teeth. She doesn't look at all like me, and she doesn't even talk like me, but occasionally she rears her ugly head. On a good note, we eventually learn to tame the beast inside. We'll get to that later.

78. You will suffer from acute memory loss.

During the initial stages of my divorce, I had a Teflon memory. I had a hard time remembering things. This is typical. You are walking around in shock and very preoccupied with your thoughts during this time. You are very self absorbed and overwhelmed with emotion. It's like someone has zapped all your memory cells out of your brain – and used them in a Keanu Reeves film for feeding the Matrix.

It is traumatic when our marriage ends. Medical studies have shown that when we are traumatized emotionally we can block things from our memory. Blocking a traumatic experience from your memory is a psychological protection mechanism; being forgetful because your mind is so overwhelmed with emotional chaos is another. There's a fine line between the two and the subject is highly debatable. I'm not sure which it was in my case, but I was traumatized that my husband would treat me the way he was, and I was forgetful because I was overwhelmed emotionally. The beginning stage is where this happens. Keeping a journal is extremely beneficial during this time. It will jog your memory and help you keep facts straight.

My wonderful mother tried to help make my life easier during this difficult period. She hired a gardener for me, so I wouldn't have to do my own yard work while taking care of my two small children. It was awesome. Then one day when things were really bad, she had made arrangements for my carpets to be cleaned. She knew it would make me happy (hey, doesn't everyone like clean carpets!), but to this day I do not remember having them cleaned. It happened. My sister, who was there with me, swears that they were cleaned. I was simply not present mentally. This was a clear reminder to me that I was still under a lot of stress, and the shock of my marriage ending had yet to completely set in.

I know this to be the case of my ex, too. During this stage, he had confided in my sister how he also was having trouble remembering things.

79. Communicate with each other as little as possible for awhile.

At the beginning stage of your divorce decisions have to be made. This is when you have to treat your divorce like a business. It's a partnership you are trying to dissolve. In business and in divorce, when someone doesn't comply with a request and/or their input is needed, there are many ways to seek a response. If you can't get a response from them verbally or in writing, then you go to a third party, and if you still get no where, you have to make assumptions on how they would respond, put it in writing and inform them that in the absence of their reply, here is what we are assuming, date stamp the sucker and send it certified mail with receipt of delivery. Chances are you will get a response.

During this time, it is best to have as little communication and contact as possible with each other. It's an anger-rich environment, and contact just adds to the stress. Our crap meters are calibrated and loaded to go. Our tolerance of their crap right now is off the chart — somewhere around negative 40.

But, with each ringing of the telephone, that panic feeling surfaces and your heart pumps faster. What if there is more bad news? What if he/she is cold to me again? Why is my spouse throwing it all away? Will this be the time I can convince them to change and come home? Do I want them to come home?

So how long is a little while to wait to communicate? It depends on if you have kids or not. If you don't have kids then after all the property is divided you won't ever have to deal with this person ever again, that's the good news. But if you do have children together, oh, the fun you will have! There is no hiding out. You'll have to communicate sooner or later with them and it is usually sooner than later. In addition to property matters, you'll have to talk about schedules, money, and possibly illnesses with the children.

Why put yourself through this? There is no moral code that says we have to answer the phone when our estranged spouse calls. If it makes you uncomfortable, then let it go to voicemail or send emails. And for goodness sake, change the voice mail message. The first step to closure is as simple as changing your outgoing voice mail message. I called a friend of mine who was recently separated from her husband and got her voice mail. Her husband had been moved out two weeks before and her message still had his voice saying, "You've reached the Bickles. Jerry, Laura, and the kids can't come to the phone right now." That was a huge clue she had not accepted it.

When you have to send the kids off, have their backpacks ready with all they'll need and set it just outside the front door. No personal appearances are necessary. You can attach notes to the back pack if necessary. When you see your ex pull up and the doorbell rings, kiss the children and send them out. When you see them arrive back home, unlock the door and then hang out in another room.

For some people this isn't possible. The potential for violence is too great. When this is the case the courts can work out an arrangement for you, but I'm talking about what to do until then. When the potential for violence is too great and you feel at risk, have a third party there to send the kids off and to receive them for you, while you go somewhere else. Pay a sitter if you must, or have a friend or relative help you until things simmer down. Sometimes just meeting in a public place makes people less free to vocalize feelings. I've seen a lot of people make the switch in McDonald's parking lots.

THE MIDDLE

Most things in life can be solved or explained through mathematics, almost everything except emotions. It's hard to say how long it takes to get to the halfway point in the divorce circle. You may feel like you will end up in a halfway house long before you get to the halfway point, but don't despair. When you know that you would never go back to your ex, no matter what, you can rejoice in knowing that you are halfway to indifference. At this stage you may still love your ex, but you know in your heart you wouldn't and couldn't go back. So celebrate for a moment; You have arrived at the point of no return, the middle. It's a monumental revelation when you realize it for the first time. It means you can free yourself and look elsewhere for love and happiness.

80. You may wobble and falter with self-doubt on occasion, but trust me, you will have an epiphany about your ex that will set you straight once and for all.

I remember waking up countless nights, knowing something was wrong – something didn't feel right. Then, like a smack in the face, I'd remember: "Oh, he's with her, and we're getting divorced." There is nothing like this rude awakening in the middle of the night. I was crying alone, thinking that Dickhead is getting it on with her, probably screwing her right now. If they had sex half as often as I thought about it, they'd be in the *Guinness Book of Records*. I couldn't understand how they could do this to me. I'm here to tell you of the benefits of masturbation. It's a harmless way of saying, "I'm getting off too and f— you. Didn't need ya anyway!" Truth of the matter is, neither one of them were ever thinking about me, and once I realized that I got mad, and finally things began to change.

My epiphany came in the form of a dream. Some time had passed, and I was getting used to calling him by his new name, Dickhead. At this point in my life, I was feeling better about myself, too. I had lost a few pounds and was exercising regularly. My motivation to exercise probably wasn't what it should have been, but nonetheless I was getting fit and looking good. I figured I had better work out for three reasons. First, I wanted to look good to make him regret leaving me. Second, you never know when you might have to kick her ass! And third, she was 12 years older than me and I wanted it to show. It's been eight years, and I still work out five days a week, but now I do it for one reason, my health.

One night I dreamt I was seducing Jim, and he wanted me back. I was dancing around him and he was getting an erection of mammoth proportion. His penis was getting so big it was starting to get uncomfortable for him. He yelled out my name and pleaded with me to stop turning him on. I continued with my dance and like a balloon blowing up larger and larger until there is nothing left to stretch, his penis exploded. It was a defining moment for me. I woke up not feeling empty or jealous anymore. In fact, I was so appalled that I never desired him ever again after that one dream. I didn't say our epiphanies had to make sense. I mean, this was pretty wacky, but it got me there and I never had to go back.

81. When you are in the middle you may still have feelings of anger, sorrow, and regret, but you know you are moving on and you feel good about it.

When I was at this point, I think I felt more sorry for my ex than anything. I was moving on and I could see that he was just coming to terms with everything. I knew he was far from where I needed him to be for us to ever reunite and I had worked out my own resolve about it. We did not pass through this stage together.

You may find that you still have heated disagreements during this stage, it may be because you are not in this stage together. When you are in the middle, your anger from these spats dissipates faster. Instead of getting rushes of adrenalin every time you have to see each other, you may actually wonder how they are doing instead. You may feel your comfort level around your ex change back to normal.

I felt good about having my life back and being in control of where my life was headed. It was like I was 23 again, but now I was wiser. I knew myself better now, I was more worldly, and I had more confidence in myself. You will reach a point where you say to yourself, I'm (a) single (parent) and I've got it going on!

THE END

Now, continue with your circle and complete it by drawing the bottom point upward in a arc until you have it, your full circle. Once you have gone full circle you will become indifferent about your ex. Not only have you freed yourself to look elsewhere for love, but you have freed them as well.

82. You will know you have gone full circle when you don't think twice about being kind to each other.

That's when you know you've gone full circle. One time, my ex was late in picking up my son, and by the time he arrived he was drunk. He had been drinking on a very hot day and had been at it for quite some time. He had driven a good distance and was obviously past the legal alcohol limit. Instead of being angry, I was truly concerned for his safety and others on the road. I offered to drive him home and when he declined, I insisted he come inside and rest. When he was able to drive, I told him to come back for our son in the morning, he agreed. Afterward, I knew we had really gone full circle to be able to do this. For me to offer him a ride home or to come inside, for him to accept, and for us not to fight about any of it was nice. It was what it was.

Divorces are rarely friendly or amicable. In fact, on the whole, they are pretty nasty. Anyone who tells you otherwise was probably clueless in the marriage, too. I never wanted to see my ex again, but because we had two children I had to deal with him. When it is forced upon you and you have to work things out one way or another, eventually both parties will succumb to the energy it takes to stay hateful. After a long period of animosity toward each other, one of you will start to bend and show kindness or even sympathy. That's when things miraculously will change.

83. You will be humbled by the power in forgiveness.

You will eventually get to indifference and when you do, you will be surprised how one act of kindness will lead to another and another. I remember very distinctly when this turned around for us. My ex had retrieved a dog from the pound. It was a breed I was not comfortable having around my children. We argued, and the conversation ended with me hanging up on him. He waited a few minutes and called me back. When I answered, he calmly asked if it would help if I met the dog and saw for myself that it was mild mannered. Although I didn't think this would solve anything, I agreed and asked if he would keep it away from the children until he got to know the animal's temperament. After trying to work out a compromise, things began to change between us. We were taking baby steps, but we started relating to each other more civilly. It was definitely a turning point.

FROM THE TUELBOX

The process of morphing your relationship from marriage to divorce requires conflict resolution skills. The irony is you didn't have these skills perfected in marriage and divorce will be no different. The School of Hard Knock has a motto: *"You are never too old to learn"*. The divorce degree program has no prerequisite class. Divorce is the crash course on conflict resolution.

Going full circle is the precursor step to having an ideal divorce. It takes a lot of time to go around this circle. You may not pass through any of the stages together with your ex, but once you have made this journey all the way around, you will find a complete change in yourself.

10

The Ideal Divorce: Is it an Oxymoron?

IF ANYONE HAD TOLD me seven years earlier that I would be happily remarried and comfortable running next to my ex on a treadmill at the local health club, I would have said, "Yeah, right, when hell freezes over." Let me just give you two clichés to live by:

1) Hell does freeze over; and
2) Stranger things have happened.

These words never rang louder than the day my ex jumped on the treadmill next to me and proceeded to run three miles with me. The amazing thing is it was no big deal to either of us by that point in our lives. We had achieved the ideal divorce – temporarily.

The idea of an ideal divorce is an oxymoron to most. Oxymorons are words that by themselves are contradictions, but when combined, have meaning such as: jumbo shrimp, pretty ugly, or friendly fire. The words "ideal" and "divorce" aren't usually used in the same sentence. The ideal divorce is just that, an ideal. Whether you believe it or not, there is such a thing, but my experience has been that it comes in waves and can be fleeting. You can achieve it and even maintain it for long periods, but all it takes is a disagreement and you're back to enemy status. The good news is truce comes much faster the longer you are divorced.

WHAT MAKES A DIVORCE IDEAL?

Three things:

1. Being flexible with each other
2. Being supportive of the children
3. Being able to get along with each other's current spouses

We all want the ideal divorce because it will save our children a lot of heartache. That's reason enough. But because we are human and divorce is an emotional process, what makes sense doesn't happen right away. We know we want to have peace, but sometimes it is impossible.

It takes time, maturity, and personal growth from both parties to reach the ideal divorce. How much? Well, in my case, a lot. It took six years. The maturity level was not reached until there was support and understanding within the context of our current relationships. And that didn't happen until he ended the relationship with the woman with whom he had had the affair. Although they did marry, the relationship ended after about five years. She could never understand his role as an involved father, and I was a bone of contention.

She and I never reached an understanding, and I'm doubtful we ever could have. Thankfully, nature took its course and their unstable relationship finally ended.

It was different for my former and current husband. Before Todd and I were married, he and my ex went toe-to-toe one night on my front porch. It was over my son. Jim was angry at Todd for carrying a point too far with my son, and Todd was mad at Jim because he jumped to conclusions. Jim was separated from his second wife and living around the corner from me when he threatened Todd to be gone by the time he came over. At this point, Todd was more involved in my children's life than their father was and he refused to leave a house that didn't even belong to Jim. Minutes later Jim rode up and Todd was waiting for him outside. They stood so close their noses almost touched. Todd is a Texan native and Jim has Native American blood. It was like a modern day western being played out between a Cowboy and an Indian. Neither threw any punches, but there was a lot of hoopin' and hollerin'.

After that night, things changed between them. They seemed to have reached an understanding. They began to see things through each other's eyes. Once they established a relationship, I was freer to extend pleasantries with my ex. After some time, those pleasantries turned into actual conversations and eventually a new type of relationship.

84. There is such a thing as the ideal divorce; If you have a forgiving heart (and the mistress hits the road) you will experience it.

Some people aren't as lucky as I was. In my case, the other woman who was the catalyst for our divorce left. It had been a matter of principle for me not to accept her, and anything nice he did for me made her angry. She was party to our divorce and insanely jealous and insecure. Once their relationship ended, things turned around for Jim and me.

My friend Sharon's catalyst never went away. The woman that contributed to her divorce has been with her ex ever since. Her ex has had to feed this woman's insecurities by being difficult with Sharon. As long as the drama with Sharon continued, he didn't have to be miserable at home.

Let me just say to those who have had adulterous affairs, you will never have the ideal divorce as long as you remain with the person who was party to your divorce. Your ex will never accept your new lover, and your lover will always feel insecure about any relationship you maintain with your ex. This, in turn, will cause your relationship with your children to suffer. I'm sorry, but that is just how it goes. You will never have an ideal divorce until you dissolve the relationship that ended your marriage.

Achieving the ideal divorce won't be on your list of priorities if you are a battered spouse or don't have children. It won't even be a priority for a cheater, at least not initially, but most divorced people want the calm it brings. Unfortunately, people don't know where to start. It is a give-and-take process, and if both aren't willing to share in the process, it won't happen. The process starts with a simple gesture –a phone call, or a compliment. A compliment turns into a conversation and then another simple gesture, and you're on your way. Remember, this is the ideal; it doesn't always work out, but at least you tried.

85. We teach those close to us how to treat our ex. If we are forgiving, they will forgive; if we are not forgiving, they will not forgive. So be careful what you say.

It was amazing how my interactions with Jim changed how my family saw him. It's funny, but after I was okay with my ex, my family started to accept him again. I learned that friends and family feed off your interactions. We teach our families when it is okay to be nice.

One morning after my parents had spent the night, my ex arrived early with the children so that I could take them to school. My parents watched with what seemed to be silent praise for how far we had come. It had been over six years since my parents and my ex had spoken or even seen each other. My parents were quite accepting of him as a person again. This is because *I* was accepting of him. Once he left the woman he left me for, he was truly a different person. He was happier, friendlier and much more flexible.

86. Divorce can give you a hemorrhoid – BIG TIME!

But it never seems to fail, just when you think you've got the Ideal Divorce thing working for you, somebody gets stupid and all good deeds go unnoticed. Divorce is like this. There are cycles of these good and bad times.

From time to time your ex might have a flair up of the Anal Cranial problem. Anal Cranial is brain damage caused by lack of oxygen when someone has their head up their rear-end too long and as a result has lost all ability to reason intelligently.

When your ex contracts a case of anal-cranial and starts acting like a hemorrhoid, it's time to introduce them to Witch Hazel. Go to your medicine cabinet and stand in front of the mirror. Tease your hair and make a face, then say, "Hocus Pocus". Witch Hazel will appear instantly to guide you.

Witch Hazel can cure Anal Cranial. She will make a horny toad out of your ex in no time flat. With the wave of her wand she can send a little notice from the courthouse, update the child support, and instill new custody orders. Her spell book is her rolodex of attorneys, paralegals, social workers, Child Protection Services, counselors, child support collection agencies, and Family Court staff. She'll have your ex wishing they never disturbed her bats.

Don't be fooled by the calmness. It's only temporary. There's always the chance it can change. Just when you think you've got the ideal divorce thing working for you, something can happen and in a flash change the tempo of your relationship. When your ex shows their ugly side you know its time to dust off your broomstick and ride by the light of the moon again.

Seldom is there a rational reason for their inconsistent behavior; it just is what it is. Disagreements will exist as long as you both are raising children together. In the beginning of my divorce when we had disagreements, it was all about who could hold out the longest and carry out their threat first. As your divorce ages the stand-offs don't seem to last as long and you realize the energy it takes to carry out any threat. You figure the other is just blowing off steam and soon you will reach an understanding. As such, the cycle ensues.

FROM THE TUELBOX

The best way to deal with the ups and downs of divorce is to develop a bad memory. Let the stuff go and try not to hang onto it for too long. The stress will eat you up if you are not careful. Realize that you can have the ideal divorce if all the conditions exist, but there is no guarantee it will last; it's cyclical. Issues come up all the time that can change these conditions if your ex is in your life on any kind of regular basis.

Every first Monday of the month the School of Hard Knocks sponsors a friendly competitive game of Divorce Dodge Ball at the local YMCA. When you're in a down cycle with your ex and need to get out your aggression, give them a call…

11

A <u>New</u> First Time for Everything

THERE WILL BE MANY "firsts" after your divorce. Maybe you've washed the dishes a few hundred times before, but there will be a first time that you wash the dishes after your divorce is final. When you look at it that way, everything you do will be a first. It's because your life is truly beginning over.

Some of these firsts will be reasons to celebrate, and some will be reasons to cry. Nonetheless, they are what bring us closer to closure.

Most of these firsts are uncomfortable for us, as it should be. After all, we are doing these things for the first time. It's like being reborn as an adult. There's no time to graduate into each phase like we do from childhood to adolescence to adulthood. You are bombarded with all the new things, and it may feel a bit overwhelming. The learning curve is steep, but as you do these things over and over, they will become familiar and natural again.

Then you change again. It starts to feel good to do things alone, such as:

- The first major purchase without your ex (not needing approval to spend money)
- The first time you have the house truly to yourself

- The first time you can decorate your house the way you want
- The first time you realize laundry for one is fun

Then something changes yet again. You realize it would be nice to have that extra load of laundry to do, or have someone around to have input on the way your house looks, or someone who cared enough to question your purchases. These are the pains of the healing process. Eventually you will find your middle ground.

This chapter will guide you through some of these uncomfortable new firsts.

THE FIRST NIGHTS ALONE IN YOUR BED

Those firsts nights alone in bed are the most restless nights of sleep you will ever have. I used to stay up as late as I could until I would just collapse. I would exhaust myself with projects around the house and hope I would be so tired that I wouldn't wake up in the middle of the night. It never failed, though; no matter how hard I tried I would always wake up.

So you lay in bed with your thoughts and your tears. The emptiness is excruciating. The only thing comforting is hope, but in those dark hours, hope seems lost. This is when our spirituality grows, and we learn to pray. My advice – don't pass up the opportunity.

THE FIRST TIME YOU GO TO COURT

Before you can have any "firsts after your divorce", you must bless the process with a court appearance. This is by far the most uncomfortable first. Sitting before a judge with your spouse is never easy. The only thing reassuring about the gala event, is you are part of a cattle call. On our court date there was a room full of other divorcing couples. It was an eye-opener, because you realize it is just another day in court for the judge and if he/she can get through most of them by lunchtime it will be a good day. You hope for an empathetic judge, but realize family court judges have heard it all. It is a humbling experience and one you never wish to repeat.

THE FIRST TIME YOU RUN
INTO YOUR EX IN PUBLIC

If you are one of the truly lucky ones, you won't have the misfortune of running into your ex in public, like me, until you are ready. If you are not so lucky and your ex has moved back into the neighborhood, it is just a matter of time before your paths will cross unexpectedly – like at the grocery store. Happy, happy, joy, joy! This happened to us at a time when things were still hot. I strolled up to the ice cream isle and who should be standing there, but Jim. There wasn't another soul around just the two of us. Jim had obviously come to the store just for the one item - ice cream. He had a small basket, while I was doing my weekly shopping. Picking out ice cream is something that takes a little time, so we both stood there staring at the ice cream. Finally I broke the silence and said hi. I received a very trite hello back. It made choosing my flavor that more difficult. So I grabbed a carton and moved on to finish my shopping. It's one thing to cross paths in an isle, but it was quite another to get stuck behind each other in the checkout line and act as if we didn't know each other.

Perhaps your ex doesn't live in your neighborhood, but the potential for seeing him or her at one of your children's sporting events is a very real-and-present danger. I say danger tongue-in-cheek, but to those whose wounds are still very raw, this can be an extremely uncomfortable event especially if you were the one who did not want the divorce. I remember I used to feel physically ill before going to one of my children's functions. I was so afraid of seeing my ex and possibly the new woman in his life.

Yes, we could avoid the situation entirely and just not let our children attend these functions, but they are the ones that lose in the end. So for their sake, we have to muster up the courage and force ourselves to be strong and do the right thing.

The experience of running into your ex in public before you are healed is a very unpleasant one. It is a nerve-rattling experience to say the least, especially if they are not alone and have their new someone with them, but you are stronger than you think.

We basically have three options when we run into our ex with their new someone. One, we can dodge the bullet and high tail it out of there; two, we can hide; and three, we can make our presence known.

Most people would choose to avoid any communication. But here is how you can shine in this situation. Let's face it, we all describe our ex's as somewhat abnormal to our friends. It helps us cope. Our ex's do it about us, too. They tell their friends how we are off our rocker. So your number one goal is to appear very normal, not quirky. If your ex is alone, your goal is still the same – to remain normal and calm.

THE FIRST TIME YOU REALIZE YOUR EX IS STILL YOUR EMERGENCY CONTACT PERSON

There are so many financial, medical, and household things we have to get in order after our divorce that it is easy to forget a thing or two. There's nothing like the sphincter shrinker we get when we realize we haven't changed important papers that still contain our ex as the contact person. Realizing our ex still

holds power of attorney for life support should we become
hospitalized and comatose, or that they are the emergency
contact person should we be involved in an accident, isn't a
laughing matter. Some of you may be puckering right now!

THE FIRST TIME YOUR EX
COMMITS AN ACT OF LARCENY

Let me just say this, protect, protect, protect. Whether you
believe it or not, if you reside in the residence you and your
ex shared and your ex has moved out, there is the chance
that even after a petition for divorce has been filed they will
try to "get a few of their things". And why wouldn't they if
you haven't changed the locks or scrambled the garage door
remote? It's not a matter of "if," but "when" they will try this
and you will feel incredibly violated.

My girlfriend explained it to me like this. "I even felt
violated after my ex entered my house just to give me a
birthday card. There, next to the chocolate cake I made,
was his card wishing me a happy birthday with a note that
said farewell. I was peeved more than anything that he could
just waltz right into my house when I wasn't home. It made
me wonder how many other times he was there without my
knowledge."

My dear cousin went through a similar situation, only her
ex came over to pick up a few things out of the garage. He
had called her and, when she didn't answer, left a message
that he was "swinging by", knowing full well she was at work
and wouldn't be there. He still had the garage door remote
nine months after he moved out and well after the petition
for divorce was served. At this point he had his own place
complete with a new girlfriend, yet he still felt he had this
right.

In general, larceny is defined as the taking and carrying
away of the property of another without the consent of the

rightful owner, with the intent to permanently deprive him or her of the property taken. It is considered either a misdemeanor or a felony depending on the value of the property taken. So, if there is no live communication and no agreed upon items to be taken, and no permission to enter the home, then to me that sounds and smells like some degree of larceny – and you don't want to "go there" with the ex.

It is so vitally important to protect yourself for peace of mind. A few of my top recommendations include:

1. Install an alarm system (most alarm companies will work with you on a price if you tell them your circumstances.)
2. Change the garage door remote code. In the meantime, lock your garage door at night. There is a lock switch on the manual operation bottom on most openers. Make sure all members of the family know how to unlock it incase there is ever an emergency to exit the house.
3. Change your locks. All of them (house and car).
4. Install a mail slot in your door or wall near your door. You will want all your mail safely inside, inaccessible to anyone but you.
5. Take a self defense class or two.

THE FIRST HOLIDAY WITHOUT YOUR EX

The changing of the seasons that lead to the first holidays without your ex will seem bittersweet. Depending on the reasons for the failed marriage, holidays may not have been a fun time for you. Your perspective on the holidays may change.

THE FIRST LONG DISTANCE TRIP YOU TAKE ALONE

Taking a trip alone can be a little scary if you've never traveled by yourself. At times, it can even be down right lonely. It's all about being in the right frame of mind. You have to look at it as an adventure and be open to things as they come. It can be an extremely liberating thing to do. If traveling alone makes you nervous, travel with a group. There is safety in numbers, and there are all kinds of traveling clubs you can join. You may even make some lasting friendships. If you do travel alone and are in a foreign country it is a good idea to carry some cash on you. You never know when you might have to bribe a crooked taxi cab driver.

THE FIRST DATE AFTER YOUR DIVORCE

Here you go. You've just accepted your first date for coffee, and suddenly you are flooded with emotions. You're already having second thoughts. You didn't expect this. It will pass. It is just the first date jitters. Just remember it is only coffee!

You accepted the date because you wanted to convince yourself you are moving forward. A good date will prove that, but you've just convinced yourself you are not even interested in this person. So now what? Do you keep the date or cancel it? You are afraid. You are afraid they may like you and worse yet, you may end up liking them. And before you know it, you have visualized yourself married again! Yikes! Who wouldn't want to cancel the date, turn tail and run? But don't sabotage it this way. Just keep repeating, "It's only coffee. It's only coffee!" The cool thing about coffee is that it is still morning by the time the date is over. You don't have to contend with the awkward goodnight kiss.

Okay, so now you've done the coffee date, and it's time to advance to the first dinner date. Don't panic. Repeat after me, "It's only dinner. It's only dinner." But let's be honest. The real reason we are nervous and scared is we fear we will be seduced.

I surveyed 100 people who had either been divorced or who had been in long term relationships that ended and asked them several questions about "re-entry" dating. One question I asked was, "When going on a date, which is a bigger concern to you: Will there be sexual playtime? Or, what will I wear? 23% wondered more about sexual playtime and 77% wondered more about what to wear. The fact that it was top of mind for almost 25% of the people surveyed indicates that when we are on a date, one of us is most likely thinking about being seduced.

In your mind you've already played out the entire date. Right or wrong, it ends with your first naked encounter since your marriage. You've never had a one nightstand before, and certainly that's all this would be, but that goes against your morals, or does it? It used to anyway, but things are different for you now. You are not easy, you are not cheap, and you are not needy. You *are* independent, you *are* 30/40 something, and you *are* horny. So you decide to go with the flow and whatever happens, happens. You're an adult after all. It is this dilemma that psyches us out the most when it comes to the first date.

The biggest question is: Is tonight the night? Will I get lucky and get a little? By not setting any boundaries for yourself you give up your control. If you choose to go with the flow, that's okay, but if you truly want to eliminate those jitters, visualize the end of the date and what you want, or don't want to happen. And whether the date ends at the doorstep or the bedroom should be of your choosing.

THE FIRST MEAL YOU COOK FOR SOMEONE ELSE

For a woman, there's just something about cooking for a man. If she is not healed from the scorn of her ex, being asked to cook is asking too much too soon. She will be offended and may even add that she hasn't cooked for another man since her husband, i.e., "What the hell makes you think I will cook for you when I just met you."

I remember when an ex-boyfriend from high school found out I was single. At first I was flattered that he would come by and help me with a few things, but then when he said he takes payment in the form of a good dinner, I nearly slammed the phone down and took out my cootie spray. The poor soul didn't know. He was thinking, "It's only dinner," and I was thinking, "Sure, first dinner, then sex." I would have happily paid him money for all his troubles, but the idea of cooking for him turned my stomach. I ended up finding someone I could pay instead. All women aren't like me, but at that particular point in time I wasn't recovered enough to even toy with the idea of cooking for another man, let alone having sex with him.

THE FIRST NAKED ENCOUNTER
AND THE FIBRILLATER FRIEND

Concerns about the first naked encounter are vastly different for men and women. Women fear sharing the site of their bodies. Many of us have had children and inwardly know, the old gray mare just ain't what she used to be, but in time this inhibition subsides. For men it's a performance thing. Men wonder if women will think they are suave and have concerns whether or not they can please her.

87. You will be hyper emotional and sensitive for a period. Cartoons will make you cry.

During my first naked encounter with someone new, I wept the entire time, but back then I would cry at cartoons and commercials. That tells you how ready I was. I was an emotional wreck. Fortunately, he was a friend and just held me.

We usually choose a friend for our first naked encounter, someone safe, just to jump-start our heart again. A fibrillater friend is sometimes just what the doctor ordered.

Even though this person is a friend to us, we know and they know we are not soul mates. When everyone is on the same page, this can be the pseudo relationship that pulls us through this stage.

THE FIRST TIME YOU INTRODUCE
YOUR NEW SQUEEZE AS YOUR EX

Todd had been in my life long enough for my sisters to be all a buzz about the new man I was dating. It was my niece's birthday, and we were on our way over to my sister's house for cake and ice cream. In the span of the four blocks to my sister's house I rehearsed the introduction in my head. So when she greeted us at the door I gave her a big, "Hi, this is Jim." After which she corrected me and said, "Good one, way to go, I think you mean Todd." Like older siblings do, I gave her an opening and she ran with it until the minute we left.

There have been countless other times I have said Jim's name when I meant Todd's. It is embarrassing every time, but it happens. And when it does, just acknowledge you're a nut case and move on. Then try never to do it again.

THE FIRST TIME YOU HEAR
YOUR EX HAS REMARRIED

No matter how long you have been divorced, hearing that your ex has remarried can send a jolt through you. I have heard of cases where people who have been divorced for several years still feel a twinge when they hear this news. Fleeting as it may be, it is still hard.

Of course, the less time you have been divorced the more the news stings. In my case, we had only been divorced for three weeks when I found out he had remarried. When his sister called to tell me she had some bad news about him, I thought she was going to tell me he had been in an accident. When she finished, I think I could have handled the news about an accident better.

No one in his family knew about his marriage until it was over. I never will forget everyone's shock, needless to say my own, when they heard the news. His mother told me she was in the drive thru line at Wendy's when after ordering her food she paused to ponder what he had done. She stopped to pay for her food and then in a dither kept on driving through forgetting her food. When I heard the news it was as if my internal battery went dead. Although I knew our marriage had ended, I wasn't ready for the news. The finality of our divorce was summed up by that one act.

FROM THE TUELBOX

Most likely your reference to doing things as a single person ended in your early twenties, until this point. In your thirties or forties you typically have a lot more of your affairs in order, and you have a better idea of who you are, so there's more to enjoy about having "it" to do over again - until you realize that "it" involves dating.

This may be an uncomfortable phase, but if you can be adaptable you will have a fighting chance. It's the 'No Pain, No Gain' principle to moving forward. Unfortunately, it doesn't stop here. Get ready to turn the page as I welcome you to the world of post-divorce dating. Hang tight for this next ride!

12

THE GENERAL RULES
What Every "Re-Entry Dater" Should Know

THE GENERAL RULES FOR divorce etiquette and "re-entry" dating are like the general rules in life. They are the unwritten codes of conduct that most of us understand, but don't always abide. For example, if you are feeling fat, don't talk about how fat you are around someone who is fatter. That sort of thing. We all understand that you don't wear your slippers to the bus stop or around town, for that matter. You don't walk up to someone's front yard and start picking fruit off their trees; you don't pick your nose or pop a zit while in traffic, and you don't name your kid "Osama."

As kids we all played the "Not it!" game. This was the game that we played to pick the one who had to do the seeking in the game of *Hide and Go Seek*. It went like this. Everyone would be bored with the present game, and in a flash it was decided that a game of *Hide and Go Seek* was in order. Without warning, someone shouts, "1,2,3" and then like popcorn everyone in earshot chimes in "Not it, not it, not it." Then, the last kid – the clueless one, the one who was winning the other game – looks up from the game board and at that moment, everyone shouts, "You're it!," and runs off to hide, leaving the clueless kid holding the dice.

In theory, you should only lose the "Not it!" game once. The trick (and the lesson in life) is to be clued in and in tune with the rest of the world around you. Often times we are the last ones to know our world is about to change. We weren't clued into the "1,2,3" warning. We missed or ignored it completely. When our lives are turned upside down, we are usually unprepared for what is about to happen next. Whether we are the one leaving or the one being left, we all feel like the one who got stuck holding the dice.

During and after a divorce, it is easy to feel like you are the kid who keeps losing the "Not it!" game. The secret to success is in awareness. So to help you get a jump on the rest of the world, let me give you some of the rules.

GENERAL RULES FOR DIVORCE ETTIQUETE

GENERAL RULES TO WINNING AT DIVORCE

We think it's all about who gets the most stuff and that that person is the one who was most dedicated to the marriage. So in fighting for the "stuff" (the cars, the house, the furniture, etc.) we believe we are fighting for valor and principle. We fight for the money naturally, but part of it is also about who was right and who was wrong. What we don't realize at the time, though, is that we will end up giving most of it to goodwill and that we both played a part in the divorce.

GENERAL RULES FOR THE PEOPLE WE HAVE TO TELL ABOUT OUR DIVORCE

Invariably, the time will come when you have to tell certain people about your failing marriage. These people include friends, family, teachers, coaches, business partners, and bosses. My general rule with everyone except friends and family is don't offer up too much. Stick to why they need to know about it and what specifically they can do to help. Then, get off the subject. For example, teachers may need to know so that they can help your children through this difficult time and understand their mood swings. Coaches need to know for communication purposes, instead of making one call, they need to make two. Bosses need to know at some point so they will understand why you are on edge and possibly lighten your workload for a period.

GENERAL RULES FOR MAJOR ILLNESS OF A CHILD

It is a hard spot to be in when your child is ill and you aren't on speaking terms with the ex. My ex and I actually had a coming together over one of our sick children. My son was vomiting for five days straight and couldn't hold anything down. During this time he was with his father, and I was on the sidelines. Finally, I asked if I could come over and sit with him. I brought medicine and 7-Up. I had been in contact with the doctor and was relaying symptoms to the advice nurse. I stayed with my son under his father's roof for part of the evening. It was a little awkward because I had never been beyond the doorstep, but I knew that just being there would make my son feel better. And it did.

My situation was not that complicated, but for others it could be. When there is a jealous girlfriend or spouse who might not appreciate your involvement then it's time to have a little "come to Jesus" talk and break it down to them. If you share legal custody that means you have this right at any time. Understand, I am not talking about barging in when your child has a minor cold or flu, I'm talking about assessing the child for hospitalization and proper medical treatment.

For a child, just having the empathy of the other parent can be a wonder drug. My ex could have refused to let me come over. It could have been ugly, but it wasn't. This can be a turning point for some divorced couples. It may start the process of one kind act leading to another.

Fortunately for me, my new husband understood my mothering instincts and supported my desire to be with my son, while my ex-husband was willing to meet me halfway. I believe most concerned parents make these concessions to put their differences aside for the good of the child. I hope that will be your experience.

GENERAL RULES FOR DYING EX-RELATIVES

Just because you and your ex don't get along is no reason you should have to stop getting along with his or her family. Whenever there is a death in the family, always do the right thing and send a sympathy card or flowers. Showing up for the funeral is a touchy subject, but there are other ways to show your last respects.

GENERAL RULES FOR THE RE-ENTRY DATER

GENERAL RULES FOR A FIRST DATE

What is ironic is that by the end of our divorce we crave companionship, but the reality is we are not ready for another relationship, even if we think we are. It is a Catch-22. We want to date, but the chances of being successful depend on how you define success. If that means having sex, then a meaningful relationship isn't in your plans, and by your own definition you will probably be successful. But, if successful dating to you means finding your soul mate, then odds of that happening greatly increase when you seek to understand your own shortcomings first. Most divorced people learn this after they've been doing the dating thing for awhile. They know that it takes time to rediscover themselves and realign their priorities.

In the prior chapter we talked about how uncomfortable that first date can be. This chapter will provide some guidelines for normal first date behavior for the 30/40 and over crowd.

SURVEY

As mentioned in the previous chapter, I conducted a survey of 100 people who were either divorced or had been in a serious relationship that ended. I asked them some pretty personal questions about dating after divorce. Here's what I learned.

When asked "Are newly divorced people something to run from or something to be sought after?" 80 percent of the participants answered that they felt newly divorced people are something to run from. The remaining 20 percent did not feel that way. Many sited that the "newly divorced" need time to heal and resolve their own issues.

So you're out of the gates and dating again. You've been out of the dating scene for ages and are clueless about the rules. What are the boundaries and who's writing the manual anyway? You need to know.

Relax. Everybody out there was once in your shoes. That is, of course, if the feet in those shoes you are dating aren't 20 or 30 years younger than you. For the most part, everyone is on an equal playing field. Some have been playing the game longer and are more perceptive than you may think. Remember you are in uncharted waters and sharks lurk for prey like you. Dating after divorce is a lot like learning to scuba dive; you might just want to start out snorkeling on the surface before you put on the oxygen tank and go for the deep blue water.

RULE #1: *WHAT YOU SHOULD WEAR*

The general rule is to act your age and dress age appropriately. If you need some help, just comb through a Spiegel or JC Penney catalog for some ideas. Go to a department store and see what's on display. Ask for help. Sales associates love a dating mission. Polish your shoes, and bring breath mints. For men, trim all probing facial hair and unibrows. Pull out the tweezers, for goodness sakes. Ladies too! Now go and have fun. Damn kids!

Just whatever you do, don't wear a camel toe. A camel toe is a fashion faux pas. It is something little known to most women, but widely known to men. It is probably one of the few fashion rules most women don't even know about. A Camel Toe is the effect you get when you wear slacks that are too tight that lift and separate everything. The visual effect from the front is the appearance of a camel's toe in the crotch. We see this a lot with spandex attire. And with today's spandex blends, we are seeing more and more camel toes walking around. Slacks with give are the best thing since acrylic nails, but girls there's no room in the city for camels.

RULE #2: *THE FIRST DATE SHOULD NOT LAST LONGER THAN TWO MEALS*

A general rule is that the first date should not exceed the length of 2 meals. You can pick which meals, but I still recommend starting with just coffee. This date is commonly called the "Meet and Greet" date. It is short and sweet, and if you hit it off, it could turn into lunch. And if the date isn't going anywhere, you can save your money and get on with your day. It is just safer that way.

RULE #3: *ALWAYS HAVE A PLAN "B"*

If you learned nothing else from your divorce, you should have learned to always have a Plan B. This is a must! Anyone who has survived a divorce has had to kick Plan B into overdrive at one time or another. Plan B is what paid the mortgage the first month after you were separated. Plan B is what got you through when alcohol was not an option! So when it comes to dating, always have someone waiting or something to do later. Have a friend call and check in to see if you need rescuing in case the date is a dud.

This is why I never recommend dinner for the first date. If you are the one paying, it can get costly. Spending money on people you will never see again or who may not appreciate you or the dinner is a bad investment. Spend your money wisely and keep the first date short and sweet.

RULE #4: *DO YOUR CLUB RESEARCH.*

If you are at all like me, your first naked encounter came way before you actually took off your clothes. I'm talking about that first blast of humility you get when you walk into a bar for the first time in ages. Suddenly the Emperor has no clothes and tag, "you're the Emperor!" You wonder, "Am I blind? Why don't I see people here my own age?" You scour the crowd in vain hoping to find people older than you. A good rule of thumb is if you've never heard the music they are playing, then you are probably in the wrong bar. Better places to go are hotel chains that cater to an older crowd for dinner and dancing.

RULE #5: *TOPICS TO AVOID*

If you just raked your ex over the coals, don't brag about it. That kind of stuff has no place for impressing a potential date. It won't be funny to them. Chances are either they themselves were, or someone they know was, screwed in a divorce unfairly, and you become an easy target. Avoid talking about your troubles on a first date, period!

RULE #6: *ALWAYS KNOW YOUR WHY*

Knowing why you are going out can help you determine the type of person you want to date. For example, if you want to do more traveling, you might want to find a person who likes similar adventures. If you want to do more investing, you might want to date someone who is also looking for additional income streams.

RULE #7: *ALWAYS SEEK TO UNDERSTAND THEIR "WHY"*

It is wise to understand what brought this person to you. Why are they dating, and what are they looking for in a person? How many times have you heard dating is like a job interview? You are looking for a good fit, and you can only do this by asking the right questions. Though you may never come right out and ask, you may want to cleverly investigate through conversation the following questions.

"Job" Interview Questions	Translation
1. What qualifies you for this job?	1. Why should I be interested in you?
2. What experience have you had and how long was your last assignment?	2. Have you ever been married and how long did it last?
3. What are your goals?	3. Do you work and will you pull your own weight?
4. What are your expectations of the job?	4. Let's see if you say what I want to hear.
5. What salary are you seeking?	5. Are you looking for a meal ticket?
6. How do you handle work force diversity?	6. Have you done a lot of dating since your divorce and do you have a string of ex's still coming around?

WHAT THE RE-ENTRY DATER
SHOULD WATCH OUT FOR

You need to get used to the swing of dating. Things are not altogether familiar at first. What you thought worked in your 20s may not work for you now. Besides how long ago was that, a decade or two? The whole scene is different now. I met my first husband at 23, at which age I had very little life experience. So when I got divorced nine years later, I had a lot of catching up to do to learn the ways of a brave new world. Here are some of the lessons and principles I had to learn. Hopefully this will help you meet and grow with that special someone.

RUSHING

When a relationship is new, everyone is on their best behavior and intentions of being a good partner are 110 percent. Moreover, when the sex is good, a new couple can't get enough of each other. They enjoy each other's company and want to spend a lot of time together. Pretty soon they know each other's schedules and calendars and are thrown into an unspoken commitment. Suddenly when one person needs space and the relationship it halted, the one left behind feels used. These kinds of romances beg for air. When no space is built into the relationship, it is safe to say it began with neediness. If this situation is all too familiar, then my next bit of advice may shock you. This wouldn't happen if everyone would just settle down and get out of heat!

88. Don't let your sexual activity exceed your level of commitment.

Relationships need time to flourish and grow. Most new couples have to endure some bumps in the road before a relationship hits it's best cruising speed. So many people think "not rushing" means waiting a month or two to have sex. Not so. Not rushing things means waiting to get to know the other person before you have sex. That can take much longer than two months. In today's dating scene, waiting this long would seem abnormal to most people. That's because our society is so impatient, and the expectation is that if you haven't "gotten any" by the third date, there must be something wrong. Avoid this trap. Patience is a very old fashioned virtue and one not practiced very often any more.

When Tony met Tina, he decided he wanted to take things slow. He knew too well his track record with women. If he jumped into bed with her, he would lose interest in about six-week's time and would be ready to move on to someone else. He confided in Tina how he wanted to take his time and get to know her before they had sex. Tina thought this was very romantic, and she agreed to wait. But after a couple of months, Tina began to wonder if Tony was still attracted to her. He would tell her she was pretty, but she was becoming impatient and insecure. Tony would reassure her and after nine months he was able to move forward with a sexual relationship with Tina.

Tina later admitted that although their relationship was void of sexual intimacy for nine months, they became even more intimate doing other things together, like laundry, going on a hike, walking on the beach, even eating dinner. This worked so well, they knew the rewards of waiting to have sex would be even sweeter when it did finally happen. By not rushing into sex and getting to know each other first their relationship was based on friendship and not just sex.

IMPLIED/UNSPOKEN COMMITMENTS—IT'S A TRAP

In my book, you are not committed to anyone until you have talked about whether it is a mutual commitment. If you feel like playing the field for awhile, then do that and don't feel guilty. The general rule here is: Make no assumptions when it comes to commitments. Commitments are not implied at this stage in life. This is difficult for the newly divorced because once you have been divorced, you seek comfort in absolutes, and knowing where you stand in your new relationship is one of them. Be careful, though, because this can frighten people who have been single for a long time. You could come across as needy.

Too often when commitments are implied, a misunderstanding is certain to happen and one person ends up getting hurt. So before you speak to your partner about wanting a commitment, ask yourself, "What do I want?" Do I want to keep it light with Brian and see what happens with Rich, or do I want to jump back into another serious relationship? If the goal is to find yourself but have companionship along the way, then now is not the right time to be committed to anyone except yourself.

Try not to confuse having sex with someone as the "implied commitment." That's *the trap* for both men and women. Ask yourself this question: "Would you buy a house without researching the market?" Probably not. You're going to see what else is out there, run a few comparables, see what fits your budget, check out the location, etc. People who don't invest the time to really define what it is they are looking for in a relationship, wind up settling for that property near the substation. You should have fun during this phase of your life. You finally have that second chance you so boldly worked to achieve. Don't give up the farm too quickly. Do your relationship research!

KNOW WHEN TO REVEAL SENSITIVE ISSUES

Everyone has skeletons in their closets. The general rule about revealing those old bones is this: Excavate slowly. Think of it this way, whenever you hear of a major archeological find, you hear about all the exploration that came first and how long it took to hit the mother lode. When dating, we feel compelled to tell our love interest all about our past, immediately. It's not necessary, reveal slowly. According to my survey, most people agreed that there is definitely a right time and a wrong time for the "reveal." In my survey I asked when you should reveal you have the following to a new potential partner:

1. You have children
2. You have had a bankruptcy
3. You are recovering from an addiction
4. You have a sexually transmitted disease (STD)
5. You are separated

All response choices were the same for each question. The choices were either the 1st, 2nd, 3rd date or just before or after the 1st sexual encounter.

84% Said you should reveal you have children by the 1st date.

62% Said you should reveal you have a bankruptcy by the 3rd date.

40% Said you should reveal you have an addiction by the 3rd date.

50% Said you should reveal you have an STD just before 1st sexual encounter.

85% Said you should reveal you are separated by the 1st date.

FORWARD WOMEN VS. SCARED MEN

As women age and develop a sense of who they are, they start to take charge of their own lives. They've had to in order to get to this point. So when it comes to dating, they don't know any differently. I think women who have to make a lot of decisions in their day-to-day lives might be labeled "forward" or "aggressive." To successful women, these labels are accepted in the business world, and it is hard for them to turn that characteristic off when it comes to dating.

Women don't need to turn the switch off, just tone it down a bit and use it appropriately. Many men have told me they like women to make decisions about where they go, once in awhile. Those are the operative words, "once in awhile", but not all the time. Men get confused by an aggressive pursuer. Sure men are flattered, but it's a fine, very fine line, that can be easily crossed.

A male friend of mine in his 30s made the observation that it was an epidemic with successful women in his age group. He said they are so much more forward than they were when he was twenty-something. From personal experience, I can tell you this, women who are perceived as being forward just don't want to waste their time.

The reason forward women scare most men is that it simply goes against what most men have been taught. Women need to understand this. Men seem to be scared by women who go overboard with something thoughtful before there is an established relationship. For example, Stacy was just starting to date Eric when he told her he had a job interview coming up. Stacey thought she would do something thoughtful and take a small gift to him with a card wishing him well. When she set it on his doorstep and went to leave, Eric looked out his window and saw her driving away. He immediately thought she was checking up on him. He had not walked outside his door yet to see her package, and when he did, he still felt funny about her not announcing herself. Their relationship was too new for this. Men are not naturally edgy; they just don't like surprises in the beginning of a relationship.

My friend said that women who want to play the field without strings attached are even more forward. He said it is almost like a role reversal. He said he could only handle them if he was on the same page and wanted the same thing, too. To him the problem was that after getting a taste of sex, these women just wanted more. Again, it is a little backwards from the time-honored tradition of men always taking the lead on the path to sex. Women can still get their message across without being forward. But it's an art and takes practice.

FISHING OFF THE PIER

If you have never heard the expression "fishing off the pier," it simply means looking for a mate in the workplace. Allow me to tell you why this is a bad idea, from my personal observations. In the first place, the office is a place of business, not romance.

89. If you are party to a love triangle at work, everyone will know and will talk about your personal business. It is professional suicide.

Dating someone from work can make your work day more fun and exciting, but if it doesn't work out, be prepared to see your ex with someone new at work. Office romances have no room for jealously and are very unforgiving when they don't work out. You will be forced to see that person, whether you want to or not. You may even have to work on a team together with their new honey. The initiator of an office romance should practice extreme caution, given today's sexual harassment laws. If you initiate repeatedly at work, you will get a reputation. And believe me, word will get around.

THE GAME OF CATCH AND RELEASE

As a child, you probably played the game of tag. Tag is survival of the fittest for kids. If you could run fast, you didn't have to be "it" for long, but if you couldn't run very fast, you were usually "it" for the duration of the game. The object of the game was to chase the others until they were close enough to touch or catch. Once you were caught, you had to run after the others and tag the next person.

Tag is a game of chase. As kids, it was the thrill of not getting caught. As an adult, the thrill of the chase is in getting caught. It usually means you are the one chosen for a roll in the hay and then after that you are let go.

Catch and release is the adult's version of tag. It is most often played at big parties, weddings, events or large social gatherings. The game begins with the offer of a drink to a stranger. If the stranger accepts the chase is over. Next is the nonintellectual conversation about the obvious, that later turns to sexual innuendos. Pretty soon the innuendos become personal suggestions. Let me show you how it goes, "This drink is making me so horny." This is code for, "I want you to screw my brains out." As the evening progresses, an offer of midnight company ensues and before long the two are engaged in play. The release follows much flipping and flopping.

Let's not kid around, people sometimes only go to parties for one thing. It's to play the game of Catch and Release. And if you think people pay big bucks to go to big charity events for the sake of being charitable, think again. It's for the chance to play the game. How you react to this game will depend on your openness for it.

187 Things I Learned AFTER My Divorce

INTERNET DATING

90. Internet dating is a step above a blind date.

Who do you complain to when no love connection is made on a blind date? The friend who set you up, right? Anyone who has ever been set up by a friend knows it is done with good intentions, but when it doesn't work out, it can be a little uncomfortable. As well-meaning as friends are when match-making, there is something to be said about anonymity when dating.

Internet dating is good because you can prescreen your own date. But don't be naive. What you see isn't always what you get. How truthful are people when they post their profiles on the Internet? How can you be sure the self-proclaimed knock-out blonde is a knock-out, or a rich dude is really rich and is in fact a dude? The same caution that applies at a nightclub needs to be practiced online. People are just as likely to falsify their income, marital status, and employment, online as offline.

Internet dating is a pretty disposable way to weed through people. And some people can be down right cold. My friend Rick has three kids. He met a girl on the Internet, and they starting emailing. Next thing you know, he invited her to dinner at a nice restaurant on the American River. As they started to get to know each other, the question and answer phase began. She wanted to know what he did for a living and his marital stats. Like a trouper, he answered all her questions honestly. When she asked about kids, Rick knew this was a sensitive issue, but he wasn't hesitant to reveal that he had three beautiful children. He and his kids were a package deal. This news just about sent her to the river's edge. When Rick recounted this story, he told me how angry she was at him for wasting her time and not telling her about his three kids sooner. With that she set her drink down and wished him well.

Before Internet dating, there were the personal ads which always seemed to have a desperate connotation associated with them. But now Internet romance activities are much more mainstream than ever. According to PEW/Internet's survey, people are connecting online in a number of ways such as: flirting, dating Web sites, asking someone out on a date, and finding a destination to meet someone. In addition, their study found that 31% of American adults say they know someone who has used a dating website and 15% of American adults – about 30 million people – say they know someone who has been in a long-term relationship or married someone he or she met online.

66% of people I polled said they view people who do Internet dating as Adventurous.

33% of people I polled said they view people who do Internet dating as Desperate.

My numbers were very close to an independent national survey conducted by PEW/Internet on Online Dating. In their March 5, 2006 study they found that 61% of online adults do not think that people who use online dating are "desperate."

Internet dating gives you the chance to experience a lot of different people you might not ordinarily get to meet in a very short period of time, and it helps keep your dance card full on what might otherwise be a boring Saturday night. It's still fairly new, and there are many success stories, but what we haven't heard yet is how many of these marriages end in divorce? It may still be too soon to tell.

Even with these kinds of numbers most Internet users believe online dating is dangerous because it puts personal information online. When meeting someone offline for the

first time is it a good idea to practice some common sense
rules of dating:

- Meet in a public place
- Do some background research on your date before
  you meet (even if it means paying for a background
  check)
- Ask for photos
- Ask for phone numbers
- Trust your gut instinct

THE BIG TEST FOR MR. AND MRS. RIGHT

We all look for security (financial, emotional, spiritual,
etc.), but until we experience life together with someone,
we aren't fully clued into what that security is. Only time and
experience together reveals this sense to us.

The Big Test is that unspoken awareness you have about
your partner's character. In my first marriage I never really
felt secure in knowing that if something ever happened to
me, and I became sick or disabled, that he would do everything he could for me. But, when I married Todd, I never
wondered about this. I always knew without a doubt that he
would be there for me. I felt this way because I felt secure in
his love. It wasn't until I had this feeling that I knew to pay
attention to it and how important it was to have.

Every relationship leading up to your soul mate helps
define what security means to you. So what's your Big Test?

RELATIONSHIP END-ITS

There are things we do either subconsciously or
consciously to end our relationships. It is important to
understand that not all post-divorce relationships are equal,

and the reasons for their ending can seem unclear to us if
we are the one dumped.

The reasons for ending a marriage or young love are
obvious to most everyone (see the End-It Quadrant that
follows), but the reasons why our post-divorce relationships
end before they ever get started can be less obvious. Sometimes new relationships aren't really relationships at all;
they are "sexships" instead. To help you understand what I
mean, I have mapped out an End-It Quadrant and provided
the subtleties that will end most Rebound relationships and
Relationships of Convenience. But first, let me define the
Rebounder and what the Relationship of Convenience is
all about.

THE REBOUNDER SEXSHIP

Rebound relationships are based on sex and companionship, henceforth, it is a "sexship". The rebounder is usually
the first person we have a pseudo-relationship with after a
major break up. If they are clued in, the rebounder will
know their status and will proceed with caution. So here's
the tip: Being the rebounder is risky and is best left to people
who want to fill a temporary void in someone's life. The
rebounder should realize there is no future in this relationship. It is what it is.

The trouble with being the rebounder is the rebounder
may not realize they are one. Naturally, rebounders may
not be too understanding when you suddenly tell them you
might have unresolved feelings for your ex.

So how do you avoid becoming the rebounder? Ask the
simple question, "What would you do if your ex came back
tomorrow?" (For a discussion on this please turn back to
Chapter 7). As a rebounder, to avoid any surprises, it is good
to get dialed in right away on where you stand. Your first clue
is where you fall on your partner's post-divorce relationship

list. If you are the first person they have dated, chances are you are the rebounder. Wise rebounders give their partners plenty of time and space, and they don't rush into anything, including sex, if they want the relationship to last.

THE RELATIONSHIP OF CONVENIENCE SEXSHIP

The relationship of convenience is a "sexship" too and is based on one thing, sex. This relationship works well with two people who are comfortable with each other, but don't ever want a relationship together and they are both clear on that. Relationships of convenience can end when one party is no longer available for the bootie call (see chapter 7) or the enjoyment of sex with that person runs out.

If you were involved in what you thought was a relationship and it ended suddenly, perhaps what you were in wasn't a relationship at all. Maybe it was a "sexship". The End-It Quadrant might be a good place to start for finding out that answer.

Typical End-Its for relationships and sexships are listed below. Perhaps one of these hits home for you.

THE "END-IT" QUADRANT

Marriage End-its	Rebounder End-its (clues to the rebounder)	Relationship of Convenience End-its	Young Love End-its
• Cheating • Dishonesty • Loss of trust • Lack of respect • Abuse • Mental illness • Addiction • Outgrow Spouse • Control • Financial stupidity	• No talk of future • Inflexibility • Paying your own way (This will end it for female rebounders.) • Talking about an ex-lover just after naked playtime	• Acts of jealousy • Talk of commitment • Questioning • Asking for an overnight drawer • Not being available for bootie call • Calling too much	• School • Distance • Parents

DEATH BY CANDLELIGHT – THE LAST SUPPER

So much dating is centered around dining. Most of us have experienced either an engagement or a break-up at the dinner table. Having a relationship status-check at the dinner table is a sure fire way to turn a good meal bad, or in some cases, a bad dinner good. Depending on the circumstances, the last supper can be an effective way to end a relationship. That was the case with my sister who was fed up with her loser boyfriend.

My sister dated a guy in college who irritated every one he met. His mannerisms were enough to make you want to hit him with a big DUH slap upside the head. He was a big dopey guy who thought he was the eternal frat boy. They were on the outs, but he had no clue that she was getting ready to dump him. Still not quite sure what to do about their relationship, she played the role of the good girlfriend and had dinner ready for him when he got to his apartment after "working all day." His idea of working was slamming a few drinks at lunch and a few more on the way home.

She had worked hard to create a masterpiece on a college girl's budget. The table was set and the candles were lit, but he was late. When he finally exploded into the apartment, he gave her a big sloppy hard kiss, pinched her butt and clumsily sat down to the table. With one look at her creation, he mustered all his tact and asked, "What the fuck is this?"

Her reply was simple and succinct, "It's the last damn meal I ever cook for you!" With that she cocked her head, got up from the table and left the relationship forever.

Paul Simon wrote a song about 50 Ways to Leave Your Lover. According to his song you just

"Hop on the bus, Gus, don't need to discuss much, just drop off the key, Lee, and get yourself free..."

I've got one way of my own to add.

Got dinner ready, Freddie, don't need to eat it, just put it in park, Clark, sit there and listen to me...

This goes down as one of the most classic last supper stories I have ever heard. But over the years my friends have shared a number of these relationship-ending dinner experiences with me.

A friend of mine used to refer to her boyfriends by some adjective that fit their first name and personality. There was crazy and hyper Neon Deon, Hawaii-bound Maui Mitch, and muscle man Workout Willie. One fellow, Bar-b-que Ben, was a guy she met shortly after her divorce, at a bar-b-que hosted by a mutual friend. When Ben called her for a date shortly after the bar-b-que, she really wasn't ready for a relationship, but she forced herself to go out with him anyway. The date turned into more than she expected. Soon Ben was calling and coming by more than she wanted. Even though she no longer wanted to date him, she hadn't learned yet how to end it. One dinner date in particular was the turning point. She had agreed to cook him dinner for his birthday, and even though she wanted to call it off, she felt badly because, after all, it was his birthday. When he called late that afternoon to let her know he wanted to have a beer with a few buddies, she accommodatingly said, "Oh, go. Have a good time. We'll do this another night." He asked if she really didn't mind, and, of course, she was thrilled to death to be relieved of the obligation. After that, he never called back and the relationship ended indirectly over his last supper. The point is sometimes you can be gutless and still succeed at getting your point across over dinner.

FROM THE TUELBOX

Making the Dean's List at the School of Hard Knocks', Divorce Degree Program is not easy. Your GPA is based on your post-divorce dating IQ. The more you know about the General Rules the better your chances of making the Deans List. C's bring degrees, but A's will bring honor!

13

Relationship Retardation
How We Sabotage Our Relationships

L IFE IS TRIAL AND error. Some things we innately know
before we experience them firsthand, and then other
things we have to live through to fully appreciate what the
universe has to teach us. Divorce is one of those things. I
have heard a number of people who left a marriage later
say they regret ever leaving. What they find out is that no
matter how mature they were or how long they waited to
get married, it's still full of challenges. In hindsight they say
they would have been better off working things out the first
time around.

Whether we are giving up on an old relationship or
starting a new one, when we don't take the time to heal
properly we will continue to sabotage our relationship and
live with regrets. This chapter will provide you some helpful
insight on how to cure yourself of Relationship Attention
Deficit Disorder.

RELATIONSHIP ATTENTION DEFICIT DISORDER

When you were younger and you only had one love, that
first love defined all others. It became your benchmark for
love. As you grow older, many of your past love experiences

can cloud your judgment of future loves. You lose part of your innocence and love can become less defined.

91. Until you break the cycle you will continue to suffer from Relationship-ADD.

Relationship-ADD comes from having too many loves or loving the wrong way for too long. When your benchmark love is slightly off center and you have learned to love the wrong way since adolescence, you can suffer a lifetime with Relationship-ADD. It becomes a cycle of loving and healing the wrong way. When you keep going through relationships, one right after another, and don't take the proper time to learn about yourself and commit to making changes you will never break the cycle and you will continue to suffer from Relationship-ADD.

92. When you are not healed, you do not think rationally, and you can not calm yourself out of your thoughts, so you will take stupid risks with your new relationships.

We can sometimes sabotage our new relationships when we are not fully healed from our last one. Often when you are happy again and start to feel like you are becoming vulnerable, you will let your insecurities get the better of you. We all do stupid things in the name of caution.

If there ever was a sensitive spot in your last relationship from which you are not fully healed, you will find a way to make it an issue in your new relationship. Take it from one who knows.

When I was first dating Todd, I felt vulnerable to him after we had been intimate. In hindsight, I still had a lot of baggage from being betrayed. It was a sensitive spot for me, and I was afraid. I didn't know just how afraid I was at the time. I remember accusing him of cheating on me because he was late one evening. Because I felt second in some way that night and because he didn't come onto me, I thought he was up to something. The next day I accused him of cheating. He got so upset that he wouldn't see me for awhile. I was hurt for feeling that he had cheated on me, but it was a risk I was willing to take. I knew the outcome would not be good, and I felt terrible for accusing him, but it was something I had to get out in the open. I lacked trust. Todd thought I was nuts and wondered if he really wanted to be in a relationship with someone with this huge hang up. Fortunately, when we eventually spoke, he realized I was still carrying some major baggage and was willing to still see me, if we could take it slow.

Having this insight might save you from making the same mistake in your new relationship, depending on if you are the sender or receiver of an illegitimate accusation.

THE AMBUSH BREAKUP

Dawn and Dave are another example. Dawn and Dave's relationship was blossoming into a very close bond, one of love and mutual respect. They spent wonderful weekends together, going on long bike rides and taking in the simple joy of each other's company. They had been dating for five months, when suddenly Dawn phoned Dave almost in tears and said she wanted to end the relationship. Dawn was unhappy because Dave wasn't giving her his full attention, and she wanted to feel like his number one priority. Dave was heartbroken and stunned. Dave loved Dawn and was always juggling his busy schedule to be with her. So when she said he wasn't doing enough, he was terribly crushed. What Dave did not know is how Dawn had felt ignored in her past relationship. It was a familiar pain that was magnified in her new relationship with Dave. Dawn's insecurity was sabotaging their relationship.

We affectionately call this the Ambush Breakup. The Ambush Breakup comes out of nowhere and is sudden and quick. Everyone who is coming out of a long-term relationship suffers from a little Relationship ADD during this time of recovery.

THE RELATIONSHIP-ADD TEST

Relationship-ADD can be self-diagnosed. I have developed a short test to see if you or someone you know might have the affliction.

1. Do you accuse your current lover for no apparent reason of having the same failings (i.e. cheating, drinking, passive aggression, abusive behavior, etc.) as your last spouse?
2. Do you scare off potential partners by giving the sorted details of the way your ex is crazy with jealousy and has a gun permit?
3. Do you reveal too much about your vindictive tendencies by candidly sharing how much you paid for your last private investigator?
4. Do you openly make derogatory statements about the opposite sex *to* the opposite sex?
5. When asked what the happiest day of your life was, do you volunteer that it was the day you framed your ex and had him or her put in the slammer for good?
6. Do you make it a practice to secretly carry on sexual relations with more than one person at a time?
7. Do you practice the ABC method of dating? Your A person is your number one person, B is your number 2, and C is your number 3. A doesn't know about B and C. B knows about A, but not C. C knows about A and B, but is okay with it because C has his or her own ABC list too!

8. Do you need someone in your life for your sexual gratification at all times regardless of your interest in that person?

9. Do you pick someone to have a relationship with based solely on the zinger you get from their looks?

10. Do you lose interest in your sexual partner after about six weeks?

11. Do you consider two weeks between relationships as ample time for closure?

12. Do you think dressing for the occasion means dressing so that later that night you can undress on stage?

13. Do you secretly want to be a porn star?

14. Do you think if you tell everyone how great you are over and over, they will eventually believe it?

15. Do you want a new boat and plan to name it *Babe Magnet* or *Midlife Crisis*?

If you answered "yes" to any of these questions, you might have trouble landing a loving relationship. Read on and see what keeps you from achieving lasting love.

AVOID BECOMING A HUMAN YIELD SIGN

93. I thought when my marriage ended I had walked away from the problem, but the problem still followed me around.

You may have walked away from your problem, but is it still following you around? It's like that straggling piece of toilet paper stuck to your shoe. Other divorced people can see it clinging to you, even though you may not. It's called baggage, my friend. Take the case of the Human Yield Sign.

IT'S ALWAYS AN EXPERIENCE AT WAL-MART:
THE HUMAN YIELD SIGN

Wal-Mart is one of my favorite stores to shop for consumable goods, not people. I love the savings you can get there, but I love thrift stores too. It's only natural that I would love Wal-Mart. I know Wal-Mart is not for everybody. It is definitely an experience every time I go there, and the thing about Wal-Mart in a big metropolitan city is you have to be ready for just about anything. There's been times when I've almost gotten into a scuffle over claiming what was rightfully mine, like my car. There was the time when an ex-con woman, who was rather hardcore, plowed her way ahead of me in line...and that was okay, she could have hurt me. There is always the eye-witness to the verbal child abuse in the next row over, and then there are the numerous classless acts to spot throughout the shopping experience. The Wal-Mart in my city is a great place to teach your kids street smarts.

The return counter is always a favorite line of mine at Wal-Mart. One night I needed to return a small $5.00 item. Because it was raining, I thought the line would be short. Wrong. But I decided to get it over with anyway. So here I am next in line, when the lone cashier's computer goes down. Behind me is Mr. Stands-Too-Close, who whispers in my ear that I am pretty. Okay, it's been raining, I have no lipstick on, I'm drenched, and my breath could be mistaken for something that lives in a barn, and this guy, who has me trapped, finds this an opportune moment to make a pass at me. I was so frustrated, I was amused. One whiff of my breath and I was sure he would leave me alone. But he didn't. He proceeded to ask my name, if I lived around here, if I came here a lot, if I was married, and if I had children – age, measurements, and bank account number were surely next on his list. I figured it was just easier to be cordial. So, for each question he asked me, I returned the favor. When I asked him how many children he had, he stammered at first and then said, "Probably eight."

94. It's never really a good idea to date someone who can't get an accurate head count on their offspring.

"Probably?" I was shocked. "Does he just not really know," I wondered. "Are there more he doesn't know about? What kind of answer was 'probably'?" Hands down this one trumped all my other Wal-Mart experiences. I had to laugh out loud. I laughed so hard, I had him laughing, too. I think the other women in line were about to applaud my patience, but they started laughing, too. I could tell this man liked women. He was not bad looking either, and I could see how his quirky charm might have resulted in eight kids. This guy was a human yield sign to women. A word to the wise is to remember: "All that glitters is not gold."

95. Give yourself at least two years of relationship-free time to find yourself again.

I'm not saying don't date. I'm saying don't get involved in another serious relationship for at least this long. While talking to many of my survey participants, many agreed that most divorced people need about two years to figure out their issues or get their lives back. Having this belief they told me they would be less likely to consider a serious relationship with someone just getting out of a marriage. The reason for this is that you're not on the other side yet developmentally. Don't despair, this doesn't mean you won't get a date. It just means you may have to practice patience in your relationships.

History tends to repeat itself, and if you don't address your own issues, you are prone to make the same mistakes in future relationships. If you jump back into a serious relationship with someone before you have had time to figure out your contribution to the breakup of your marriage, you will end up repeating yourself. You will pick the same personality type for a relationship, and you will fall back into the same tendencies and roles as before. You basically need two years of self discovery to break your bad habits and go through detox.

GIVING UP YOUR FREEDOM TOO SOON

At the end of a marriage and the start of your single life, there is a liberation period. This is typically the time when you want to see how many dates you can get and how many people you can juggle at once. You need this period of validation from the opposite sex. You see this in men going through mid-life crisis. Women do this, too, but in a more subtle way. (See chapter 14, Sex Economics 101) For women on the rebound it's more about men with money. They've tried the "marry for love" thing, and now they want to experience the "love for money" thing. But this is what happens. When they realize that money can't buy love and that quantity sex with someone younger can't compare to quality sex with someone compatible, this new found liberation can be overshadowed by loneliness. People will succumb to the loneliness, forgetting why they fought the divorce battle. They end up surrendering their new found freedom before the declaration of independence ever gets a chance to be signed.

RUSHING – What Happens When You Aren't As Ready As You Think You Are

96. Not getting closure is like only finishing half a prescription. Your symptoms will come back.

This is self-sabotaging behavior. The ending of a serious relationship can be shattering. You go though a grieving period and then try to move on. When you rush into another serious relationship too soon after the last one, you don't allow the dirt to settle.

We are all a little dangerous when we come out of a serious relationship. We are on the rebound. It is at this time that people tend to be a little selfish, too. The most selfish thing to do is to jump into bed with someone when you just ended a relationship. It is naïve to expect that you are fully recovered from your past relationship. It is even more naïve for your new partner (known as the rebounder) to expect you to be recovered. The sex may be great, but it can just get in the way later.

Even when you wisely wait to begin a new relationship, there is no guarantee that someone from your past will not cast indecision on your feelings for this new person. However, by approaching the new relationship slowly it allows you to work out any unresolved feelings and issues from your past relationship.

Unresolved feelings have a strange way of popping up at the weirdest times. I remember dating a guy and being transfixed with his feet. They seemed foreign to me. I remember thinking, those aren't my ex's feet. It was then that I knew I still had a problem. We were embracing and he was barefooted. I remember looking down and realizing I wasn't in the moment. In my mind I had been in the arms of my ex. The sight of his feet brought me back to reality and when I pulled away I wanted to run.

If you haven't achieved closure, it is inevitable that the past will haunt you. But, if you have been honest with yourself and your new partner, the two of you should be able to work through it. If your relationship is strong and based on friendship first, you can get the closure you need in a mature way. However, if it is not, you can expect continued pain and heartache on one side and confusion and neediness on the other.

SETTLING – RELATIONSHIP PLATE TECTONICS

When people hastily jump into another relationship without ample time for closure or to resolve their issues, settling happens. I call this relationship plate tectonics. Everything may look quiet, but jumping into another serious relationship too soon is like waiting for an earthquake to happen.

What happens if your emotional wounds have not properly been dealt with from your last relationship? Like dirt that over time settles and compacts every time the earth shifts, people think that the next person to come along will fill the gaps of their loss. It is not so. Getting closure and dealing with your own issues is so immensely important. It is self destructive not to seek it.

97. You know when you've settled, but it's the biggest secret you keep.

Coming to terms with this truth in your marriage is frightening, but it happens and it is more common than you think. The problem is most people don't come to this conclusion alone. Usually an outside influence—a love interest will cause the great divide. It is one thing to come to the conclusion on your own, it is another to wait for someone else to convince you of it. If you wait for someone else to convince you that you settled, then you may be disguising your own weakness and falsely concluding.

I knew early on that I had settled in my first marriage. Every time my friends spoke of their marriages and the things they had in common with their husbands, I knew then my marriage wasn't all I had hoped it would be.

HOW GOOD IS YOUR PICKER, NOT YOUR PECKER

98. If you've never really, I mean really tried, to connect with someone on a different level (intellectual, spiritual, emotional), give it a try and watch how their beauty blossoms right before your eyes.

Everyone who has been single at one time or another knows what it's like to have friends try and set you up on a date. When you do agree to a set up, how often have you been disappointed? You've got to stop and ask yourself why they keep setting you up with people who are not your type? Maybe that's because you are being lead around by the wrong homing device! Maybe you rely too heavily on physical attraction at first, instead of being attracted to someone on other levels, e.g., intellectual, emotional, or spiritual.

Making a connection with someone on one of these levels is a beautiful thing. You hear about emotional connections everyday when someone's life is saved by another, or when someone says something that touches our soul.

EVERYBODY WANTS TO FIND THEIR SOUL MATE, BUT DO YOU HAVE SOUL?

Let's face it, if you suffer from Relationship-ADD your chances of finding your soul mate are slim. You have some work to do. When you are sincere about finding lasting love, you will project sincerity. Though unspoken, it will be heard.

99. If you are ever to find your soul mate you must first be in touch with your own soul.

By that I mean, what moves you? What gives you goose bumps in life? What energizes you? What are your priorities and what are your beliefs? How do people remember you? These are the things that define your soul.

When you can define yourself in this way, you are more in touch with your soul. Some people are motivated by causes to help others, others by the desire to please, and still others by challenges. Ask yourself what motivates you? Being more aware of who you are increases the chances of finding your soul mate.

The coming together of two hearts can happen in the simplest of moments. When one soul recognizes another like soul, it is magic. When I first met my current husband, my soul knew immediately. It was like nothing I had ever experienced. I was standing in a doorway watching him, and I remember thinking to myself, "Darn it, I'm going to like him." I was just starting to like being alone, and then, without warning, it was over. My soul knew before I did.

I was attracted to his soul first and then his looks. Two weeks after he touched my soul, my heart felt the attraction. What does that mean, you ask? During that initial two week period of seeing Todd more and in different clothes, different situations, and studying him, my heart began to feel the attraction. But how he touched my soul is a different story – that was instantaneous.

Ask anyone who has ever experienced the soul connection and they will tell you very specifically when and where they were and what they were doing. Todd touched my soul through my 3-year old daughter. As I stood in the doorway to my kitchen I watched him practice tying his shoes with her. It was that simple. The strange thing about it is, you could ask 100 different men to perform that simple act and it would not mean anything other than grown men tying their shoes with a 3-year old. So why was it so significant to me when Todd did it? I don't honestly know, but I can tell you that fate had a lot to do with it.

Like every good tale, there is a story behind this story. Prior to meeting Todd I had briefly dated a guy in construction. One day he was trying to be helpful and unscrewed the drain line to my water heater. In protest I told him not to mess with it. It was old and had never been drained. It caused a slow leak and over a couple months caused some major damage.

Not everyone believes in fate, but I do. Todd was my claims adjuster and I felt that fate had sent him to me. It was a Monday afternoon and he came to inspect the damage my water heater was causing.

Having a soul attraction is different from a physical attraction. The best way I can explain the difference is that a soul attraction will scare you. It's that pivotal moment you swallow hard and think to yourself, "Uh-oh what's that I'm feeling?"

FROM THE TUELBOX

Everyone is afflicted with some degree of Relationship-ADD. Making the change within ourselves is key. Recognizing that it will take some time is paramount.

14

Sex Economics 101:
The Pig Theory

YEE-HA! YOU ARE FREE at last. Greener pastures, here you come! No barriers, no fences for this little squealer in the middle of a corn field. No, sir-ee. For awhile, it is great. For the not so discriminating, you can have all the sex you want. You can visit the adult bookstores all you want. You can rent as many adult movies as you want. You can have as many partners as you want.

WHY IT'S GREAT TO BE A PIG

For a Pig, gluttony is the name of the game . . . variety is the spice of life. Non-committal sex is like trying all the chocolates in the candy box and spitting out the ones you don't like. Being a pig means you can have recreational sex with a variety of age groups. And best of all, you don't have to be accountable to anyone. This is a very common phase divorcees go through (both male and female) immediately after a divorce. It's as if you are making up for lost time. You cram everything in you didn't do, because you got married, into this next phase of life. Some may feel a little slighted, a little gypped by getting married so young and not getting enough time to "play the field". To them now is the time to run with the ball. Others may feel this way because sex was used as a weapon in the relationship.

ESTABLISHING THAT YOU ARE A PIG

It is only fair to be completely honest that you are in pig mode. You will spare yourself a lot of headaches if you are upfront with others, too, because here's what happens when you aren't honest: you get caught. Soon after the pig gets sent to the slaughterhouse.

Here's how you announce you are in pig mode. You say, "I just want to let you know I'm going through a phase, and I don't want any commitments; Now, let's have sex." And if you score, you successfully achieved Pig status.

PIG FRIENDS

To help you be successful with your pig status, I have a few tips on whom you should solicit. The pig keeps friends with other barnyard characters and marine life. Some of the pig's best friends are Horsey Whore, Never Say No Nelly, More Than Once Marey, Horny Toad, Stanley Steer, and Moe B. Dick. To the pig there's nothing hotter than someone coming out of divorce. The pig knows the newly divorced just want sex (because odds are they haven't had any for awhile). Accordingly, the pig will scam the market for those fresh out of the gates.

Red Alert. You don't want to be stuck in this phase for too long. There's nothing worse than an ignorant pig. Being a pig can be fun for a little while, but according to my survey, the general public only puts up with this act for about twelve months. Friends may even think it's good for you for a little while, but if you are going to be a pig for more than the somewhat socially acceptable timeframe, make sure to get your head examined (both heads for you guys) and be safe about it.

UNDERSTANDING THE PIG

It's a numbers game with the male pig. It's all about how many women they can get. Women go through the Pig phase too, but it's not a numbers game, per se. It is about acquisitions, but not of the gender kind. Women that go through the Pig phase use it to their advantage. Here's the difference between men and women on the Pig Theory. Female pigs have several motive operands (M.O.'s) when it comes to dating, male pigs have one. They are as follows:

The Female Pig's M.O.	vs.	The Male Pig's M.O.
Free Gifts		Sex
Male Attention		Sex
Entertainment		Sex
Escape from cooking		Sex
Excuse to get dressed up		Sex
Sex		Sex

After coming out of divorce I've come to appreciate why so many people fall into the Pig phase. Here are just a few reasons why...

- The Pig realizes it would not be good for them to have a relationship right now. The Pig knows this about him or herself and should be commended.
- The Pig lacked validation within his/her marriage and during this time needs to be validated by the opposite sex. It's a game he or she must win for their own self-worth.
- The pig realizes this might be the last time in their life to express their sexual freedom and still be young

enough to get away with it. The problem is, the pig is in denial about his or her true age and fails to realize they are not 21 any more.

Male Pigs past the age of 40 are not subtle. They will come right out and tell a woman that they want to have her *and* her friend. Older female Pigs are also open and direct. They will call a pig, a pig to his face, then consider the request.

For the victims of Pigs, understand, you usually don't have to worry about the Pig staying the night. Few pigs risk getting sucked into spending the entire next day with you.

Pigs have bad memories. Few will ever remember your phone number or details about you.

ANDY ROONEY'S UPDATE

I love to listen to CBS's 60 Minutes with Andy Rooney. Here's what he has to say to all those guys out there who say, "Why buy the cow when you can get the milk for free": *"Nowadays 80 percent of women are against marriage, why? Because women realize it's not worth buying an entire Pig just to get a little sausage."*

THE MILK IS NEVER FREE - WHY IT'S SMARTER FOR THE PIG TO SWITCH TO SOY

If you really believe the milk is free then you're living under a rock and you need to pull your head out fast. I'm here to tell you the milk is never free, there is always some kind of price to pay for casual sex. Yet, the pig's not too bright. The pig still thinks that sex is a bargain to be had. The poor stupid little fool thinks sex is free. Just ask Hugh

Hefner how much it costs to keep three girlfriends happy on spa day.

Pigs that think they're getting the milk for free have all been duped. Male pigs pay for sex in obvious ways such as: paying for a meal; bearing gifts; and paying for entertainment. Female pigs are more subtle. She pays for sex indirectly by purchasing sexy lingerie and spiked heels, maintaining herself in top form (hair, nails, and makeup), for the extra tank of gas she will spend being the designated driver, and for the extra fattening food she keeps in the house to feed her male counterpart, but if she is a true pig she will work it so he pays for everything.

Soy milk is a substitute for cow's milk and comes from the soy bean plant. Soy milk is to cow's milk what masturbation is to sex. "Dipping your cookies" takes on a whole new meaning with soy. Bottom line, there is no substitute for sex, but when you switch to soy there isn't any "cow" to buy, and you can safely get what you need using the alternative. Just something for you to keep in mind.

THE TWO-PUMP CHIMP - THE SURPRISING TRUTH ABOUT MASTURBATION

I never will forget the time I chaperoned by daughter's third-grade class on a fieldtrip to the city zoo. One of our first stops was the primates' cage. A zoo docent led the tour. She was an elderly lady and very knowledgeable about all the animals. She was in the middle of explaining a particular chimpanzee's aggressive behavior when he paraded his way up a limb, stopped in the corner of his cage facing the children and began to fondle himself to the point of an ejaculation, all in a matter of seconds. The other mothers and I were horrified at what our children had witnessed. To our relief, in their innocence they did not know what had just taken place. Our grimaces and disgusted looks all too quickly turned into smirks and hidden laughter when one of the mothers exclaimed she captured the exhibition on video and to come look at it again.

We were all so astonished not only by this chimp's lack of decency, but by the fact that primates masturbate. In her educational description of what had happened, our docent discretely explained to the parents that masturbation was a very common act among the primates at the zoo. I had no idea that such an act was so primitive and so instinctual. I had to stop and think, "If we are like them and they are like us..." It was all starting to make sense. It partly explained why some men are such exhibitionists with their genitalia.

PIG ECONOMICS: WHEN IT'S CHEAPER TO PAY FOR A HOOKER

Sex is never going to go on sale. It's not likely you'll ever see a clearance rack for it in the back of a department store (even in Nevada!). I suppose if you ever did, you wouldn't feel comfortable with what you got anyway. It might be last year's style and may have been tried on a few too many times. So let me help you with this one.

The way we are taught to value shop and compare is like this: volume per unit price. The larger the ratio, the better the deal. In other words, what is the unit cost when you buy in bulk? Here's an example: Which is the better buy, a dozen eggs for $2.40 or 6 eggs for $1.80? The unit price for the dozen eggs individually is the same as 1 egg for 20 cents each. However, the unit price for the 6 eggs individually is 30 cents each. You can see the larger the volume the greater the savings.

Another way we comparison shop is by looking at price and price alone. Sometimes we can be fooled by price alone forgetting that there might be hidden costs. For example: There are two shirts on a rack. Which is the better buy? The cotton shirt that costs $50 or the dry clean only shirt that is on sale for $25. Without any further consideration, our initial thought is the shirt for $25 because it is cheaper. But here's the thing. Let's assume it costs $5.00 every time you need to dry clean your new shirt. Five cleanings and it is just as expensive as the cotton shirt ($5 X 5 dry cleanings = $25). The next time you have to dry clean your shirt, it will cost you more than the cotton shirt. The cotton shirt is wash-and-wear and will never cost more than $50. The cotton shirt is the better buy in the long run.

Now let's put this in pig terms. Given two potential partners to have sex with, which will bring the Pig the better deal, the expensive hooker or the free sex that comes with casual dating? If we put the volume per unit price theory to practice, the hooker comes out the better value. Here's why:

Depending on the brothel house where the pig frequents, it can be safer than casual sex. By the time you pay for dinner, movie, a few drinks and gas for just a goodnight kiss; you could have had a brothel house experience. After the dirty deed, there is no emotional baggage or awkwardness either. There's no worry of future child support. You will probably never see this person again. Dollar for dollar, the experience is all about you, the Pig, after all why wouldn't it be, you paid for it. So for these reasons, it's cheaper to pay for the hooker in the long run.

Note: By no means am I advocating prostitution. This example is simply to illustrate Sex Economics and the Pig's psyche.

There are degrees of male Pigs. There are the smart ones (the brick and mortar pigs) and the dumb ones (the straw and sticks pigs). The smart pig understands Sex Economics. He doesn't make the fatal error of confusing a date for a hooker, at least not to her face, but the not so bright pig has trouble distinguishing the two. He thinks paying for the date equates to paying for sex and will treat his date like a hooker.

There are also degrees of female Pigs. There are the ones that are more than happy to fall into the hooker category, this in part explains the male pig's confusion. After all, it might be confusing to a poor dumb pig whether or not his date is a hooker based on the way she is dressed. And then there are the female Pigs that know their sexual worth and will make the poor dumb Pig spend his last dollar on her before giving up sex.

THE PIG AND THE PORN STAR

A Pig walks up to a Porn Star in a bar and says, "Hey, how can I be like you? I mean you get all the sex you want and get paid for it? I would give anything just to get lucky with one of your ladies. How does a guy like me get your job?"

The Porn Star replies, "You've got to have a big Johnson."

The Pig says," I always thought my Johnson was big, see I'll show it to you." With that he unzipped his pants and showed the Porn Star his wears.

Amused by the Pig's candor and confusion, the Porn Star whipped out his wallet and proceeded to show the Pig the engraving on his wallet. It said, "Big Johnson".

SEX ECONOMICS: SUPPLY AND DEMAND

Yes, it is nice to impress someone with a fine dinner on a romantic first date, but my theory on this is: let the romance develop over a nice afternoon walk in the park or a ride in a canoe, or a picnic. Let the demand for romance dictate the supply of it. In other words, when you overwhelm someone on a first date with too much romance, it won't seem sincere.

100. Don't invest so much of your emotions into a first date.

Sometimes people vest too much of their emotions into a first date and feel slighted when there is no connection. After about four or five first dates ending this way, you can go broke and feel rejected. When this happens you need to rethink your approach. Keep the date simple and this won't happen. Take it slow and gradually build up steam. Go for a drive, stop for a coffee or lemonade, and then call it a date. Go for a walk or a bike ride. Get back to basics and you won't go wrong.

101. Don't invest financially into a relationship before you've invested emotionally.

Let me repeat: don't invest financially into a relationship before you've invested emotionally. You wouldn't do this in business, so why do it in a new relationship? Save your money for something special with someone you know *is* special, not someone you think *will be* special.

To the pig, anyone who is willing *is* special. The smart pig knows all this and that is why he avoids any unknowns. He will make his rounds with all the sows he knows are a sure thing.

THE MARGINAL PROPENSITY FOR SEX

The marginal propensity to consume is a theory about the way we value commodities. It's based on human behavior. Let me show you how it works.

Let's say you are in Death Valley in the middle of July. The temperature on the valley floor that day is 110 degrees. Your car has broken down and you are 15 miles from the nearest trading post. So you get out of your car and start walking. You get about a quarter of a mile down the road and you think, "Man, it is hot! A beer would be really great right now."

As you keep walking, the sweat from your brow begins to drip onto your nose. You lick your lips only to taste the salt you are losing from your body. You take your shirt off and tie it around your head. You become even thirstier, but no relief is in sight. You continue walking, feeling the steaming heat. You begin to feel the symptoms of dehydration: dry mouth and no spit to swallow. After about five hours in the heat, you are spent.

Suddenly, like a mirage, you get a glimpse of a lemonade stand with shade and refreshing misters. You run, only your legs can't seem to move fast enough. You would pay anything for a sip of lemonade. When you get closer you realize it's not lemonade they're selling; It's beer - bonus! The guy at the stand knows how hot it is and that there isn't any beer around for miles. So he charges accordingly.

Your one beer will cost you $20.00. You gladly pay it without blinking an eye. He takes your money and hands you a cold one. You twist off the cap and slam it down. You are so thirsty that you buy a second beer at that price. You slam that down, too. You relish the shade and the misters. You don't want to leave. So you decide to stay awhile. You end up buying and consuming 10 beers from this guy in the course of an hour. You begin to feel sick and you know one more beer would put you over the edge. At this point you wouldn't drink another beer even if it were free.

After that 10th beer, you had reached your marginal propensity to consume. The value you received from that last beer did not have the same value you received from your first beer. It's like this with sex. You would pay big bucks for the first time to have sex after not having it for awhile. Then you might even pay a little extra just so you could do it all through the night. But by morning you wouldn't want to pay a dime for any sexual favor. You would be too exhausted and sore for another round. A hooker would have no value to you. This is known as your marginal propensity for sex.

Knowing what your marginal propensity for sex is is only important in a short supply market. Knowing what you are willing to pay in short supply is key. In other words, the more desperate you are, the more you are willing to spend for a date just to get a little action.

But the pig has a golden rule. Never let the supply drop below the demand. The pig's marginal propensity is very marginal at best. If his date cancels on Friday night at five, he's got someone else lined up by six. It doesn't matter who, just as long as it's the opposite sex and is willing. The pig will hedge the market this way. Sex is the motive operandi (M.O.).

FROM THE TUELBOX

My point is for every pig there is a sow, and if you don't want to pork a sow, stay away from the barn and wait for the market to turn. Or, do like the chimps do.

15

101 Things I Learned after My Divorce (Tomi's List)

Epilogue

Thanks for reading, *101 Things I Learned After My Divorce.* Everyone's divorce reality will be different, yet there are universal similarities we each will experience. My mission was to help those of you who landed on the same battlefield that I did and make you feel better about your life in spite of the challenges divorce brings.

Some of you are new recruits, others are on the inactive list, but one thing is certain, you never ever wish to go through another divorce. Unfortunately, 60% of us who remarry will eventually re-enlist and divorce again. Why? Because we're an all volunteer army and we didn't learn enough the first time!

Just remember, when you have the courage to look inward and grow from your shortcomings, you will blossom into something more beautiful and you will earn your stripes in life. You will become a better, kinder, and wiser person for it. Many soldiers have fallen from the battles of Heartbreak Ridge, but not you. You are a survivor, and that's an order from your Brigadier General!

We've come to our journey's end together, but that does not mean we part here. Perhaps you will recall some part of this book when you are in need of a voice of reason - that's when I hope to be there for you again.

I sincerely wish the best for you in the romance department. And from one veteran to another, perhaps you, too, will conclude, "We were just saving the best for last."

Please keep in touch.
www.tomituel.com

About the Author

Tomi Tuel graduated from college at age 22, then again at 30 – marriage, career, children, and a mortgage in between. Life had a certain order and divorce wasn't in the mix. But when her husband came down with the infamous seven-year itch, her world crumbled, yet all seemed to be ironically on track as she navigated the mine field of divorce. With little warning of the impending upheaval, she picked herself up to face the mêlée of her life and became a survivor – and a "new recruit" in Divorce War.

Tomi holds a Master's Degree from California State University, Sacramento, but her degree is not in Psychology or Counseling. In fact, she has no formal education in marriage and family counseling or psychology, but if the School of Hard Knocks passed out degrees, she would have a Ph.D. Now a battle-hardened veteran, Tomi is a self-proclaimed "girl with a mission" and her book is receiving acclaim from fellow authors and leading psychologists.

As her *101 Things* recounts, Tomi found peace after her divorce and now is a frequent speaker to audiences, large and small, on divorce recovery. She has remarried and lives with her husband and two children in Sacramento, California. *101 Things I Learned After My Divorce* is a must-read for anyone facing the many stages of divorce, or for an interested by-stander who wants to better understand the tribulations of a Divorce Warrior. So, calibrate your "Crap Meter" (chapter 4) and prepare to assault Heartbreak Ridge with Tomi as your Brigadier General leading the charge. In her debut book, Tomi's passion for inspiring and motivating those in the trenches is a genuine breath of fresh air – a survival kit when life's turns make it difficult to breathe.